Boy
on the
Lion
Throne

ཞིང་ཁྲིར་བཞུགས་པའི་བུ་ཆུང་།

BY

Elizabeth Cody Kimmel

With a foreword by His Holiness the Dalai Lama

Roaring Brook Press
NEW YORK

THE CHILDHOOD OF THE
14TH DALAI LAMA

Boy on the Lion Throne

Text copyright © 2008 by Elizabeth Cody Kimmel
Flash Point is an imprint of Roaring Brook Press, a division of Holtzbrinck Publishing
Holdings Limited Partnership.
175 Fifth Avenue, New York, New York 10010
All rights reserved

Jacket and book design by Christian Fuenfhausen
Photo research by Maggie Berkvist

Cataloging-in-Publication Data is on file at the Library of Congress

Roaring Brook Press books are available for special promotions and premiums. For
details contact: Director of Special Markets, Holtzbrinck Publishers.

Printed in the United States of America
First Edition March 2009
1 3 5 7 9 10 8 6 4 2

....

A NOTE ON PLACE NAMES

A current map will show neither the village nor the province where the Dalai
Lama was born as being within the confines of the territory delineated as "Tibet
Autonomous Region." The Tibet Autonomous Region currently comprises
approximately one third of the landmass historically claimed by Tibetans.
The village of Taktser and the province of Amdo appear today on maps in the
Chinese province of Qinghai—Taktser is located southeast of the enormous
Qinghai Lake (formerly known as Lake Kokonor).

Place names used in this account, many provided by eyewitnesses, may
not be recognized and represented on modern maps. Those interested may
find it helpful to consult the map of Tibet included in *Freedom in Exile*, the
autobiography of His Holiness the 14th Dalai Lama.

To Rev. Frank Geer and St. Philip's Church, Garrison, New York,
And to all people and places of peace

Contents

ངར་ཆག

foreword
སྔོན་བརྗོད།

CIRCUMSTANCES HAVE FORCED ME to spend the major part of my life outside Tibet. However, when I think back to my childhood, I am reminded of the very contented and spiritually fulfilling way of life that I was able to follow in my homeland. My experience in Tibet and the trials and the tribulations I have gone through since are characteristic of the array of challenges that the Tibetan people have had to face and continue to face today.

I hope that readers of this book will approach it as telling not just my own story, but also the wider history of Tibet.

Even though that story is far from over, I believe that my education in Tibet prepared me well to do whatever little I have been able to do for the sake of my land and my people.

Tenzin Gyatso
The 14th Dalai Lama

20 September 2008

Office of H.H. the Dalai Lama
Thekchen Choeling
McLeod Ganj – 176 219
Dharamsala, (H.P.)
INDIA

The flag of independent Tibet.

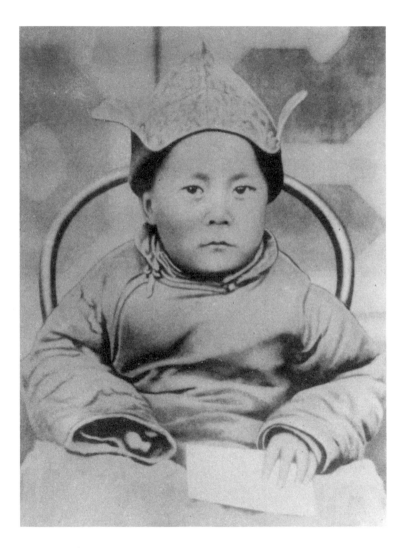

"Sera Lama"

 སེ་ར་བླ་མ།

O N A QUIET WINTER MORNING in 1937, several strangers on horseback rode into the Tibetan village of Taktser. The men made their way through the small cluster of houses and prayer shrines on the lofty hillside, searching for the one that had been described to them. They were disguised as a group of simple travelers, their true mission a tightly held secret. Through the falling snow, their attention was drawn to a farmhouse nearby. Something in the shape of the gutters around the flat roof told them this was the house they must enter. If this was in fact the place they had been seeking, the common brick-and-mud structure contained a treasure of immeasurable

....

Three-year-old Lhamo Thondup

value. The party of men approached the home. In their hands lay the future of Tibet.

Lhamo Thondup was not yet three years old when his mother welcomed the strangers into her home. The boy was immediately enchanted by the visitors, and he was especially drawn to a man dressed in a brown belted cloak and fur hat. Lhamo Thondup did not know that the servant who so captivated him was in fact the leader of the party, a high-ranking lama who had traded his scarlet monk's robes for a servant's costume.

The boy's mother, Diki Tsering, was a beautiful and gentle woman, with smiling lips and glossy black hair worn in long braids down her back. She was known for her generosity and never turned away strangers no matter what their circumstances. She offered the men a place to sleep for the night and took Lhamo into the kitchen to fetch them tea and bread. They were as welcome at her table as anyone, though she was already beginning to suspect that they were no ordinary travelers.

While the tea and bread was being served in the main room, the man dressed as a servant went into the kitchen. There he found Lhamo Thondup. When the servant sat down, Lhamo climbed into his lap and discovered that beneath the man's cloak he wore mala beads, the traditional

Tibetan rosary. The boy was fascinated by the prayer beads and wanted the servant to give them to him. Amused, the servant agreed, with one con- dition. Lhamo Thondup must identify him, though the man and boy had not met before.

mala beads

Lhamo did not hesitate. In spite of the man's clothing, the boy called him "Sera Lama," meaning a monk of the Sera Monastery. Lama Kewtsang Rinpoche was deeply impressed. Not only had the boy correctly identified the man and his monastery, but Lhamo had also shown an interest in the prayer beads. Only Kewtsang Rinpoche knew that those beads had belonged to the 13th Dalai Lama. To him, it made perfect sense that this little boy demanded he hand them over. Though there were other tests to be given, it seemed quite possible that the child on Kewtsang Rinpoche's lap was the one the search party had been seeking.

Young Lhamo could not have understood that the arrival of the party of strangers signaled the coming of great change. Life as the boy and his family knew it was about to change forever, and for Lhamo there would be no going back.

The Roof of the World

འཛམ་གླིང་ཡངས་ཐོག

L HAMO'S MOUNTAIN COMMUNITY of Taktser was a small and remote village in the Tibetan province of Amdo. Tibet has the distinction of being the highest country on the globe, with the average altitude 15,000 feet above sea level. It is sometimes called the Roof of the World and the Land of Snows.

Although Tibet is flanked by China to the east and north, and India, Bhutan, and Nepal to the south, it is also surrounded by a natural fortress of mountain ranges, including the majestic Himalayas, where Mount Everest is located. For centuries, these forbidding peaks made Tibet incredibly difficult to reach, and it is little

The borders of Tibet in 1937

wonder that the country managed to keep largely to itself. As a result, Tibet is a land shrouded in myth and was long rumored by explorers and armchair travelers to be the real location of the mystical Shangri-La—the spirit land of eternal youth.

At the heart of the country is the religion of Buddhism, which came to Tibet from India in the seventh century. Buddhism teaches what is called the Eightfold Path, which stresses living a compassionate and respectful life, doing no harm to oneself or any other living being, and keeping a clear and focused mind. It also stresses the concept of interdependence, meaning that every effect has a cause, particularly in human experience. Like all Tibetan children, Lhamo was raised to have an enormous reverence for life, not just in human form, but down to the smallest insect.

Worship was an integral part of Tibetan life. Almost every household, no matter how poor, had a small altar. Colorful prayer flags fluttered above most homes. Families prayed together after rising in the morning and before going to sleep at night. Traveling monks were welcome in any home, and the Buddhist principles of compassion ensured that most beggars would receive food or money when they asked for it.

Central to Tibetan Buddhism is the concept of reincarnation—the idea that after death a person's soul is reborn in a new body. Tibetans believe that certain teachers or lamas are *tulkus*, able to choose the manner, time, and place in which they are reborn for their next lifetimes. Once reborn, a tulku is able to continue his teachings and leadership for another generation. Though there are many tulkus, there is none more important than the Dalai Lama.

The Dalai Lama is both the spiritual and civil leader of the Tibetan people—there is no higher authority in

A group of Gelugpa monks in traditional dress, 1936

religious or political issues. Tibetans revere the Dalai Lama and consider him a god-king. Their love for and faith in him is virtually unshakable.

When one Dalai Lama dies, the country is governed by a regent, who also oversees the search for the reincarnated Dalai Lama. It is an anxious and emotional time for the Tibetan people. On that snowy morning in 1937, Tibet had been without a Dalai Lama for four years. The 13th Dalai Lama had died in 1933. Almost immediately, Kewtsang Rinpoche and other high-ranking Tibetan monks and officials had begun searching for clues to the identity and location of the boy who would be enthroned as the 14th Dalai Lama.

In keeping with tradition, the dead tulku's body had been laid out on a throne. On several occasions, witnesses reported that the face of the dead leader had turned toward the east. It was said that unusual cloud formations and dragon flowers growing near the shrine also seemed to be pointing in an easterly direction. Several important oracles turned east when seeking the location of the newly born tulku. And the regent himself, while gazing in the sacred lake of Lhamoi Latso, experienced a series of visions including letters indicating the province of

Amdo, a three-story monastery with turquoise roof tiles, and a farmhouse with a distinctive juniper gutter.

In 1937, three search parties departed from the capital city of Lhasa. Several months later, one of those teams reached the remote village of Taktser, where they encountered two-and-a-half-year-old Lhamo Thondup.

Lhamo Thondup's family would have been well aware that the search for the next Dalai Lama was under way. And like all Tibetans, they would be looking forward to the discovery with great joy and anticipation. For them, being Tibetan and being Buddhist were closely intertwined. So the discovery of a new Dalai Lama was likely to be one of the most important events that would occur in their lifetimes.

Across Tibet, monks and peasants anxiously awaited news from the search parties. Unbeknownst to them, the search party now leaving the tiny village of Taktser secretly believed they may have just found the boy the country was looking for.

Life by the House Mountain

རི་འདབས་སུ་ཁྱིམ་གྱི་འཚོ་བ།

T AKTSER WAS HEAVEN ON EARTH for a young
boy like Lhamo Thondup. The village lay in
breathtaking surroundings, protected by the towering
distant peaks of Ami-Chiri, The Mountain Which Pierces
the Sky.

About 30 small farms dotted gently sloping pastures
of lush grass. The occasional evergreen tree gave way to
forest in the distance. In the brilliant sunshine, life was
abundant. The hillsides were rich with flowers, herbs,
berries, fruits, and nuts, and a running brook nearby
teemed with goldfish. Lhamo Thondup and his family had

A typical village in the Himalayas

all that they needed—ample food and shelter and loving family and neighbors. They also had temples, prayer flags, and a *bumkhang*, a tower-shaped shrine to Buddha located near each home, for daily worship.

Lhamo's house was a comfortable dwelling made of clay bricks topped by a flat roof with juniper-wood gutters and two chimneys. A prayer flag fluttered from a flagpole. There were several rooms in the house, but the largest was the kitchen. Always warm because of the big stone stove, it was often the most popular and crowded room in the house, particularly during the winter.

In 1937, there were five children in the family—two more would come later. Daughter Tsering Dolma, born in 1919, was the eldest, followed by firstborn son Thubten Jigme Norbu, in 1922. Three more sons followed: Gyalo Thondup (1928), Lobsang Samten (1933), and finally Lhamo Thondup, in 1935. Like virtually all Tibetans, Lhamo's parents would have hoped for at least one or two of their sons to go to the local monastery to become a monk or perhaps even a great lama. When a tulku was discovered in a family, honor was brought to the entire village.

Indeed, there was already a tulku in the family. The eldest son, Thubten Jigme Norbu, had been recognized as the reincarnation of the high lama Taktser Rinpoche and had moved to the nearby Kumbum monastery. A second brother, Lobsang Samten, had also joined the monastery as a monk. The family had been blessed two times over, and in spite of the strange visitors, Diki Tsering thought it was unlikely that there was more than one tulku in her family.

Still, Diki Tsering had often remarked that Lhamo Thondup had been born with one eye wide open and did not utter a single cry. She remembered him as being an unusual child from the day of his birth. The little boy was very attached to his mother and insisted that she be the only one to handle his things. He often amused himself by packing his belongings in a bag and informing his family that he was leaving for Lhasa, the Tibetan holy city. He would draw large houses in the soil, then tell his mother that they would live in such a house. One day he announced that he had come to his family from heaven.

A typical day for Lhamo began at dawn, shortly after his parents arose. There were no clocks or electricity—time was kept by the passage of the sun. The children were supposed to be washed and dressed by the time the sunlight reached the highest mountain peaks. After morning prayers and rituals came a light breakfast of tea and *tsampa* (roasted flour balls made from special dough mixed with tea and yak butter).

Other than some light chores, such as weeding, fetching water, and collecting firewood, young boys like Lhamo were not required to spend all day doing farmwork. A lucky boy might be sent to fetch eggs from the henhouse, or even better, be allowed to follow one of the herdsmen leading cows and sheep up into the mountains. An afternoon could easily be lost in the meadows and woods, with fresh streams and ample supplies of strawberries and raspberries to keep up one's strength. There were plenty of other boys for company. And though the woods held some danger, particularly the sleek gray wolves always looking for a meal, children found safety with the herdsmen and their hefty double-edged swords.

Most children enjoyed a visit to the bumkhang. Made of clay and hollow on the inside, the bumkhang contained relics and treasures such as little statues of deities built into the clay. Sharp eyes could pick out these statues when peeking through the cracks in the walls.

Makeshift balls could be fashioned from yarn and feathers, and a small, round rock could be adapted in endless ways to suit fanciful imaginations eager to play. In

the two wet months of summer, children remained closer to home to wait out the rain.

The farmhouse's flat roof also made for a diverting play space. It provided a sweeping view of the surrounding countryside and brought a child a touch closer to Kyeri— Taktser's "house mountain."

Mountains are extremely important in Tibetan culture, and many are believed to be the homes of protective deities. Taktser's central temple was built in honor of Kyeri and the spirit the villagers believed resided there. The peak of the mountain gave the first hint of approaching weather changes, and there was no better view of it than from the roof. The roof was also a warm and protected haven, and held secrets and surprises of its own. Lhamo's brother Norbu used to

A traditional flat-roofed Tibetan house

pick wildflowers growing out of the chimneys and returned the favor by planting wild onions there.

And of course, there were always the animals. Lhamo's family had chickens, cows, sheep, horses, and a sow, along with the household dog and cat. Lhamo enjoyed fetching eggs from the henhouse and occasionally installed himself in a makeshift nest and clucked contentedly, lost in his imaginary chicken world.

Children and adults alike looked forward to feast days, and none was more exciting than the two-day celebration of Kyeri and the mountain god Kye. For the event, the entire village made a three-day journey to the foot of the mountain. There they feasted, danced, and played games. The food was plentiful. And when the adults made their pilgrimage up to the area on the mountain where ice began to form, the children remained happily behind in the tents, exhausted from hours of singing, stuffing themselves, and playing in the meadow.

Winter brought its own reward: heavy snowfall provided a perfect playground, the landscape full of natural ice slides and well decorated with snowmen. When the temperature plummeted, the snow piled high, and the wind blew bitterly, Lhamo would stay home, sitting near the stove and watching his mother work in the kitchen. At night he slept snugly, warm under layers of sheepskin. If there was anything his life or home lacked, Lhamo Thondup was not aware of it.

And yet soon he would be asked to leave it behind forever.

A King's Ransom

རྒྱལ་པོའི་བླུ་རིན།

THE SEARCH PARTY SOON RETURNED to Taktser to see Lhamo again. They had received official word from the government in Lhasa authorizing them to proceed with more tests. It was a situation that had to be handled carefully—prior to the 13th Dalai Lama, it had been over 70 years since any Dalai Lama had lived more than 20 years. Whether some were poisoned or whether they all simply suffered from diseases and accidents remains unknown. The lesson, however, was clear—whoever became the next Dalai Lama must be watched extremely closely. Along with the danger of harm from within the country was the constant threat of interference from neighboring China.

....

Four monks and a young novice stand outside the Kumbum monastery in 1937.

The traditional area of Tibet, consisting of the provinces of Kham, Amdo, and U-Tsang, sprawls over almost the entire Tibetan plateau, an area of approximately 1 million square miles. China had long been eager to establish a foothold there, and many Chinese believed that historically, Tibet had been a part of China. What had or had not been agreed on in past centuries about the sovereignty of Tibet is still in dispute. What is clear is that as the twentieth century dawned, China was keener than ever to gain influence in Tibet, as was the British-run government in India. During the reign of the 13th Dalai Lama, who lived from 1876 to 1933, Tibet had been invaded by both the British and the Manchu Empire of China. In the 1930s, a Chinese governor named Ma Pu-feng had taken control of a small portion of northeastern Amdo province, close to the Chinese border. In fact, China's influence in Amdo was significant enough that most villagers in Taktser spoke Chinese. By the time of the 13th Dalai Lama's death, Tibet was for all practical purposes independent again. But the wolves continued to circle. The future Dalai Lama would have enormous influence over Tibet's attitude toward its neighbor. Should a boy be chosen who was thought to be anti-Chinese, his life might well be in danger.

Lhamo Thondup was happily unaware of the many larger issues that surrounded the test he was about to take. When the search party presented Lhamo with the second test, the little boy didn't hesitate.

In the guest room of the farmhouse, the men arranged a variety of items. There were pairs of mala beads, ritual drums, bells, bowls, reading glasses, silver pens, and walking sticks. Of every pair of items, one had belonged to the 13th Dalai Lama and the other had not. Lhamo's instructions were simple—choose one of each pair.

Lhamo Thondup examined each pair of items and confidently chose the correct ones. When he picked up the small drum that had belonged to the 13th Dalai Lama, he began to tap it rhythmically, as a monk would during prayers. It was only when the pair of walking sticks was presented that Lhamo seemed to hesitate. He placed a hand on the first stick and examined it very closely. After several moments, he withdrew his hand and selected the other stick instead. The search team believed that Lhamo Thondup's hesitation was easy to explain—the first walking stick belonged to Kewtsang Rinpoche, but many years earlier had in fact been used by the 13th Dalai Lama as well. When the tests were concluded, the monks were more than satisfied. They reported that Lhamo Thondup had correctly chosen every item that had belonged to the 13th Dalai Lama.

Though there was much more that needed to be done before little Lhamo's status would be official, word spread in the village that the boy had been recognized as a tulku. It was whispered that he was possibly even the reincarnation of the Dalai Lama himself. During the waiting period that followed, life became less enjoyable for the young boy.

Lhamo Thondup was suddenly the object of the respect and devotion of every person in the village. At the same time, people seemed to be distancing themselves from him and his family. Lhamo wanted to continue playing with his friends as he always had, but discovered that they had all been told it was no longer appropriate for them to socialize with him. The arrival of the search party had not changed the boy's sense of himself at all—to him, everything was exactly as it should be. Unfortunately, no one around him seemed to share his feelings. All of his life, the Dalai Lama has maintained that he is just a regular person—a simple monk, as he puts it. But from the moment he passed the second test, he would never be treated like one.

Though the tests had been conducted with great secrecy, Ma Pu-feng caught wind of the rumor that the next Dalai Lama might have been discovered virtually under his nose. It certainly would have come as an enormous surprise to young Lhamo had he known that Ma Pu-feng had demanded 300,000 silver dollars before he would allow the boy to travel to Lhasa. It was a huge sum of money, a true king's ransom, amounting to more than $2 million by modern standards. Although Lhamo could not understand why he was suddenly not permitted the freedom to play outside with the other children, the reasons were clear to the search party.

Lhamo Thondup's parents were instructed to take him to the nearby Kumbum monastery, where he could be kept safe until the details of his move were sorted out. At first, the prospect of traveling to Kumbum must have seemed like good news to Lhamo. At the very least, he would be able to see his brothers Norbu and Lobsang, who were living and studying at the monastery. Neither had gotten to know their little brother—Norbu was 13 years older than Lhamo and had been in the monastery since he was eight years old. Lobsang, on the other hand, was only two years older than Lhamo but had been only three when he was taken from his home to join his brother at the Kumbum monastery.

Lhamo's parents roused him early on a freezing winter morning, and the family traveled to Kumbum, where they were reunited with their two sons. When Lhamo and his parents first arrived at the monastery, it was a happy family reunion. Then Lhamo realized that his parents meant to leave and return home to the farm without him. Though he would have his two brothers for company, he barely knew studious Norbu and quiet Lobsang and was bitterly unhappy about being left with them while his parents went home. Just three years old, Lhamo was still close to his mother.

Norbu recalls that when their parents left, Lhamo began to weep. Lobsang cried as well, leaving Norbu the job of comforting them. As a tulku, Norbu was considered to be a wise and important teacher. This distinction gave him no advantage, however, in dealing with two sobbing brothers. He did what he could to console them.

Lhamo could not cry forever. Though extremely unhappy to be parted from his mother, he gradually began to feel better. Perhaps Lobsang, who had also been separated from his mother at age three, was able to reassure him. As Lhamo slowly grew accustomed to his new surroundings, the larger issue of his becoming the next Dalai Lama, and what problems that might cause, was probably not something he gave much thought.

Lhamo soon became good friends with Lobsang. He also made friends with an old monk who treated him with great tenderness. Lhamo would climb into the monk's lap and be enfolded in his robes for warmth, happily accepting the peaches that were offered to him.

Though he preferred to spend his time with Lobsang, Lhamo was too young to join him in classes. So he spent many hours waiting for his brother to be released from his studies. He would wait restlessly outside the classroom, peering in to try and get his brother's attention without being seen by the teacher. Most of the teachers and students treated him well, with the exception of one fierce monk who happened to be his uncle. Once, Lhamo accidentally dropped the pages of his uncle's scripture, sending them every which way, and his uncle struck him in a fit of rage. In spite of such occasional unpleasantness, Lhamo gradually adapted to monastery life.

Six months later, everything changed again. A tentative agreement was reached with the Chinese governor, and it was decided that young Lhamo must be transported to Lhasa with all due haste. The departure date was set for July 1939. Frenzied preparations were made for the traveling party, which would include more than 50 people, a carriage, and 350 horses and mules.

The three-month journey would take the party through wild and remote areas of the country, and carried its own risks. The countryside had its share of wolves, bears, and bandits, and it was possible that, despite the ransom paid to Ma Pu-feng, they might still be hindered by the Chinese. To make matters worse, the plains were sometimes swept with powerful winds and storms, and the party would be sleeping in thin tents. Before they reached the safety of Lhasa, the party would have to ford rivers, ascend mountain passes, and cross marshes that could swallow a yak in mere moments. There were no real roads, only rugged caravan routes to follow.

However, most Tibetans would have gladly endured these dangers and more for the chance to see the Holy City. Lhasa was Tibet's capital, located in the south. It was also the location of the summer and winter palaces of the Dalai Lama, and of Tibet's most sacred temple—the Jokhang. Each year, countless Tibetans traveled from all over the country on religious pilgrimages to Lhasa. There was no better place to celebrate the Tibetan New Year, Losar. And in addition to the many festivals held there, Lhasa was also a hub of business, culture, and learning.

The most famous sight in Lhasa was the massive, golden-roofed Potala Palace, winter residence of the Dalai Lama. The Potala was built in the seventeenth century for the 5th Dalai Lama, though an existing pavilion there dated

Monks blow ceremonial trumpets on the roof of the Chakpori Medical College, in the distance the Potala towers over Lhasa, 1936.

back to the seventh century. The thirteen-story edifice, built high on a rocky hill, is a massive building even by today's standards, and it soars over Lhasa. In addition to containing the personal apartments of the Dalai Lama, the palace housed government offices, numerous festival halls and chapels, and a large community of monks. Rumored to have more than 1,000 rooms, it also contained priceless collections of religious scrolls and national treasures, including the remains of seven Dalai Lamas.

Well before his discovery by the search party, Lhamo had often amused his mother by packing up his belongings and telling her he was going to Lhasa. Now the fantasy had become a reality.

At last, for the first time in many months, Lhamo Thondup had something to look forward to.

The traveling party gathers in the courtyard at Kumbum in preparation for the long journey to Lhasa.

"A Happy Sun Now Shines on Tibet!"

དགའ་སྦྱུར་ཉི་མ་དེང་སྐབས་བོད་དུ་འཕོ་བ།

THE OFFICIAL ANNOUNCEMENT had not yet been made confirming that Lhamo had been recognized as the 14th Dalai Lama. But the boy himself acted as if he were certain he was an important tulku. He assured his mother that even though there were several other boys still being examined by the search party, he was the real tulku. Accounts of the journey disagree as to whether Lhamo could have known that he had been chosen as the 14th Dalai Lama. Though an official in the party believes that Lhamo's parents did not know the details of the search party's finding, Diki Tsering recalls she had already been advised by this time that her son was

---

Horsemen in ceremonial dress escort Lhamo Thondup on the final leg of his journey to Lhasa, October 1939.

definitely the tulku they sought. She was told she must keep the information to herself.

Less than a week after his fourth birthday, Lhamo packed his few belongings and said good-bye to the Kumbum monastery. Blissfully unaware of the massive amount of organization required to plan the journey, Lhamo basked in the excitement of an adventure with his family. In addition to his parents, two of his brothers would be accompanying the caravan. To his great satisfaction, six-year-old Lobsang Samten, whom Lhamo now considered his best friend, was included in the party. Lhamo's parents were also bringing their middle son, 11-year-old Gyalo Thondup. The eldest child, Tsering Dolma, had married, and because she was expecting her first child, she was unable to travel. She planned to follow the party for a day or two and then return home. Once her baby was born, she and her family would make the journey themselves to be reunited with the extended family in Lhasa. Lhamo's escort also included members of the original search party, including Kewtsang Rinpoche, pilgrims wishing to travel to Lhasa, scouts who were experts at taking groups safely through the remote landscape, and muleteers to manage the pack animals.

One family member who was not able to accompany the caravan to Lhasa was Norbu. He had cared for his brother closely during the many months the boy stayed at the monastery, but Norbu was now far too deep into his monastic studies to be permitted to leave. The teenager resented being left behind and feared that he would never see his brother again. Even as he hugged his family and said good-bye, Norbu still believed it was possible that at the last minute he too would be invited to join the caravan. But it was not to be. As the caravan moved off in the direction of a distant mountain range, Norbu stood in silence, watching. He watched as the caravan disappeared completely from sight. As he turned back toward Kumbum, tears rolled down his face. For many nights thereafter, he would think of his young brothers, imagining he could hear them calling out to him.

Lhamo Thondup was traveling in style. He sat in a specially made yellow *dreljam*, an enclosed wooden palanquin, like a sedan chair designed to be carried on the backs of two mules. Lobsang was permitted to sit in the dreljam with him. The two frequently squabbled and swatted each other, which caused the contraption to overbalance. Fearing the boys might actually overturn the palanquin, the attendants were forced to summon the boys' mother, who was being carried in her own small palanquin, to quiet them on more than one occasion.

Happily installed in his dreljam, Lhamo was probably unaware of the hardship facing the party in the early weeks of the journey. After several days of going from monastery to monastery, where they were greeted with tea and rice, the caravan approached the northern deserts. Here there was no pasture for the animals to graze. When the group camped in the land called No Grass No Water, the horses and mules suffered the lack of nourishment. But Lhamo did not have to contend with an empty stomach or a dry mouth. As always, the first priority of the caravan was the comfort and care of Lhamo and his family.

One monk attendant noticed that Lhamo tended to squabble more with his brother when they were traveling through difficult country like the northern deserts. When Lhamo cried or scowled at Lobsang, Kewtsang Rinpoche did his best to distract the brothers, riding next to the dreljam and telling jokes and stories. When the boys got bored of those, he quizzed them on the letters of the Tibetan alphabet.

Though no one was supposed to know that the caravan was transporting Tibet's next Dalai Lama, rumors spread nonetheless. People flocked to the palanquin as the party passed, but for security reasons no one was allowed near the boy. Still, they crowded as close as they could. Diki Tsering noticed that a group of tribesmen from the Sangsang village who came to greet them looked quite dirty. When she commented on it, her four-year-old son reproached her, reminding her that it was not right to judge people by their appearance.

The party advanced about 10 miles (16 km) a day, and at night attendants would pitch tents and make fires. Lhamo was roused before dawn each morning, when the air was still uncomfortably cold, and carried to his palanquin bundled against the chill. The party traveled through a wide variety of landscapes, from forests to lake lands to the high plateau, where conditions were too barren for anyone to live. Where the ground was unstable, Lhamo was removed from the dreljam and carried by one of the monks. To four-year-old Lhamo, the scenery was filled with wonders. Even the yaks and deer he spied from the window of his palanquin filled him with the sense of having encountered something extraordinary.

After two months of traveling, the party finally passed out of the reach of the Chinese governor. Safely out of

Ma Pu-feng's territory, they camped in the appropriately named Little Happy Valley. Having received official confirmation, the announcement was made in Lhasa: four-year-old Lhamo Thondup of the mountain village of Taktser had been located, tested, and proven to be the reincarnation of the 13th Dalai Lama. Word spread like wildfire. For six years, all Tibetans had awaited this moment.

It was a day that called for celebration, and the party greeted approaching Tibetan mounted border guards (called *aphors*) with great joy. Though it was still important for Lhamo to reach Lhasa as soon as possible, the group took a few hours off in the Little Happy Valley. Lhamo and his family were entertained by the visitors, who performed daring feats of horsemanship and shooting, leaping on and off their horses at full speed crying, "Ki hi hi!"

A group of about 100 government officials had left Lhasa to rendezvous with Lhamo's escort. The longest and most difficult part of the journey was over, and Lhamo's family must have been greatly relieved to learn they were now just two weeks' journey from the Holy City. Frenzied preparations were underway there for the arrival of the young tulku.

But Lhamo's attendants knew that they must remain on their guard. During one stopover several days out of

Little Happy Valley, word reached them that horsemen were gathering on the far side of a mountain pass. The attendants feared that bandits were lying in wait for them. A special guard was posted, and the caravan divided in two. Lhamo's group would not travel forward until the first group made sure there were no robbers waiting to pounce on them. To everyone's great relief, they passed through unharmed.

For much of the journey, Lhamo and his escort had traveled over countryside occupied by few people. But as the group neared Lhasa, people—monks and civilians eager for blessings—appeared whenever they stopped. Lhamo had to be on his best behavior, observing the welcoming processions and giving blessings to the many who requested them. The attention could have been overwhelming to a different child, but Lhamo seemed to take his duties in stride. To him, the real excitement lay in the beautiful countryside they were passing through. Each day brought something new. Lhamo was especially delighted when they reached the Thutob River, where a small boat floated him across the water. The brief boat journey greatly amused him, and once he was safely on the other side, he watched the caravan's horses and mules swim across.

In the village of Bumchen, the travelers met up with the advance welcoming party. The nights of camping in the rough were over. A magnificent yellow tent used by the 13th Dalai Lama had been erected. A monk carried Lhamo into the tent and dressed him in new robes of yellow-gold silk. The monk then placed the robed boy on a throne. This was not the magnificent Lion Throne that awaited him in Lhasa, but a cleverly constructed seat of earthen bricks covered by exquisite silk brocades. Lhamo had never seen anything like it before. Sitting on a throne for the first time, Lhamo was greeted by a group of high-ranking monks and members of the Tibetan government. He was presented with traditional Tibetan scarves and the Mendel tensum, a symbolic offering in three parts consisting of a golden image of the Buddha, a segment of scripture, and a miniature of a religious monument. Attendants were appointed to see to his every need. From here on, Lhamo would go from ceremony to ceremony, stopping each night to camp in his yellow tent.

The child who had until recently been a farm boy was now the center of almost unceasing attention. Had he been frightened, or fussed over losing his old clothing, his attendants probably would have understood. But Lhamo acted as if he was born to play this part, and the Tibetans believe he was.

Lhamo's parents were given the titles Great Mother and Great Father. They too were given new clothes, and Diki Tsering was presented with a pearl and coral headdress called a *patu*. Though the patu was magnificent, Diki Tsering found it uncomfortably heavy and did not wear it. She preferred the jeweled *hari* headdress traditional to her own people of Amdo. She chose to continue wearing the one she had brought with her, along with her simple *chuba*, a long, belted dress, which she had brought from home.

Now a new palanquin was prepared for Lhamo. This one was the official *phebjam* of the Dalai Lama, gilded and much more ornate than the dreljam, and carried on the backs of eight men. It was designed to carry only one person. For the rest of the journey to Lhasa, Lhamo would have to travel without his brother Lobsang. There was only one Dalai Lama, and Tibetans believed no human was his equal. This meant that for the rest of his life, there were many things Lhamo would have to do alone.

When the group resumed its journey toward Lhasa, crowds of peasants and monks flocked to greet it. From the window of his phebjam, Lhamo could see people literally dancing in the streets and weeping with happiness. Musicians played horns and flutes and clanged cymbals. Often people in the crowd would join the caravan. As the group moved closer to Lhasa, it grew considerably. Everyone clamored for the Dalai Lama. Their four-year-old god-king, perched on Kewtsang Rinpoche's lap, obliged them by tossing handfuls of blessed barley grain. The crowd was ecstatic, shouting, "A happy sun now shines on Tibet!"

The party's last major stopover was several miles outside of Lhasa, where a state reception would be held. There, a village of tents had been raised for the occasion. In the center was a magnificent yellow ceremonial tent called the Macha Chennio, the Great Peacock, named for the gilded peacocks decorating its roof-pole. At the heart of the Great Peacock tent was a towering, intricately carved wooden throne draped in fine silks of gold, red, and blue. This throne had only one purpose—to be the centerpiece in the ceremony welcoming the return of the departed Dalai Lama as a child.

Of all the new sights Lhamo had seen since leaving his home, the Great Peacock tent must have ranked among the most spectacular. He was carried to the tent in his *phebjam*,

The Great Peacock tent at Doguthang, October 1939

shaded by an umbrella of peacock feathers in shimmering greens and blues. Climbing out of his sedan chair, he proceeded solemnly into the tent, wearing splendid yellow-gold silk robes and a yellow peaked hat. A large crowd of monks and officials waited to receive the child's blessing and to offer him ceremonial scarves. They were amazed to see how calm, even serene, the boy appeared. After a full day of blessings and ceremony, however, some noticed that their young Dalai Lama was beginning to look tired.

As the party left for its final short journey to Lhasa, crowds lined the streets outside the city. To Lobsang, it seemed that every single occupant of Lhasa and the surrounding villages had come out to have a first look at his little brother. But, far from being disturbed by the sheer numbers gathering, Lhamo appeared overjoyed.

When they were close enough to see Lhasa, Diki Tsering was moved almost to tears. Like all Tibetans, she had heard tales of the great Holy City all her life. Their journey had taken more than three months of often exhausting travel. Now, she was about to enter the Holy City for the first time, not as a pilgrim, but as the mother of the new Dalai Lama. Just two years ago, the mere idea would have seemed preposterous.

Before entering the city gates, Lhamo had his first encounter with the legendary Oracle of Nechung. Because the Tibetan culture places great importance on visions, dreams, and astrology in decision making, Tibet has an official state oracle. The Oracle of Nechung's function was to provide guidance to the Dalai Lama. He did so by entering a deep trance during which he danced with spastic, jerky movements and breathed quickly in snakelike hisses. His face contorted so that his eyes bulged out beneath his massive white and gold headdress, and he brandished a sword. By many accounts, he was terrifying.

The oracle proceeded directly to the Dalai Lama's palanquin and stuck his head inside. The boy's attendants were understandably concerned that the sight of the Oracle of Nechung in full trance might frighten the four-year-old, particularly as it had already startled some of the horses. However, the boy remained calm during the encounter and placed a ceremonial scarf called a *kata* around the oracle's neck.

Lhamo's composure and grace could only reinforce the attendants' belief that he was, indeed, the reincarnation of their beloved 13th Dalai Lama. How else could they explain how comfortable the farm boy was with the lavish ritual and unceasing clamor for attention and blessings?

Once the caravan entered the city, Lhamo was taken to the Jokhang Temple. At that time, Lhamo Thondup surrendered the name he had been called since birth. In its place, he was given a string of names. He was now Jamphel Ngawang Lobsang Yeshe Tenzin Gyatso. Those close to him would address him as Kundun, meaning "the presence." The full translation of all of his names includes The Holy One, The Compassionate One, and Ocean of Wisdom.

All traces of the peasant child Lhamo Thondup were rapidly disappearing, and Kundun was springing to life in his place. After a consecration ritual at the temple, Kundun and Lobsang were delivered to their final stopping place—Norbulingka, one of the two palaces of the Dalai Lama. Traditionally, the Dalai Lama spent the warmest months at Norbulingka and the remainder of the year at the Potala Palace. The two palaces are about 3 miles apart and are often referred to as the summer palace and the winter palace. The formal ceremony that would take place in the Potala Palace to enthrone the new Dalai Lama was not scheduled until February, several months away. So it was decided that Kundun did not have to go to Potala Palace until then. The regent, Reting Rinpoche, correctly suspected that the boy would be much more comfortable at Norbulingka.

On the way to Norbulingka, the air was so rich with the scent of flowers and the atmosphere so thick with joy, Kundun felt as if he were dreaming. He had never imagined that there were so many people in the world. Even in the boisterous chaos of the crowd, he strongly felt that he had come home.

Kundun was pleased with Norbulingka, which was actually a series of buildings in a well-tended park. The winter palace, the Potala, was a massive and forbidding building, which looked gloomy and cold in the distance. But at Norbulingka there were gardens filled with fruit trees and flowers, and the palace itself was sunny and cheerful. For the time being, Kundun and Lobsang were free to play together, and the brothers roamed the gardens picking apples and pears from the trees. His family was housed nearby, and Kundun was able to see them every day. Occasionally, he indulged in quick tastes of several foods that were now forbidden to him. When a senior monk happened upon Kundun eating an egg, forbidden food for a Buddhist monk since it contained the beginnings of a living creature, both child and monk were equally shocked. Kundun reacted first, shouting "go away" in his loudest voice. While at Norbulingka, eating forbidden foods might be discreetly tolerated. Things would change soon enough.

Of his first months at Norbulingka, the Dalai Lama later said, "It was the last temporal liberty I was ever to know."

On the Lion Throne

ཤིང་ཁྲིའི་སྟེང་དུ་བཞུགས་པ།

T HE MORNING OF FEBRUARY 21, 1940, was magnificent. There was not a cloud in the sky, and the temperature was luxuriously warm. The gardens at Norbulingka must have looked tantalizing in the brilliant sunlight, but this was the day that Kundun must leave the summer palace and take up residence in the Potala.

It had been more than six years since the Lion Throne of Lhasa was last occupied. In consultation with the oracle and astrologers, the Tibetan government had determined that February 22 would be the most suitable day for the official enthronement of the 14th Dalai Lama. This coincided with Losar, the Tibetan New Year, which brought

....

Kundun is carried by sedan chair from the Potala Palace, April 1940.

thousands of monks and revelers to the city. Officials had sent invitations to the governments of China and India, to the maharajas of Bhutan and Sikkim, and to the king of Nepal. This was as far beyond their borders as they would reach to governmental outsiders—Tibet remained isolated from the rest of the world. In Europe, Nazi Germany had begun its conquest of the continent. Closer to home, Japan had spent three years attempting to conquer China, thrusting much of the world into World War II. But for the moment, the events of these dire times caused little more than a ripple in the Roof of the World.

The line of those assembled to escort little Kundun to the winter palace was more than a mile long. All were dressed in their finest clothes, and the array of silk fabrics and gems reflected every color of the rainbow. The air was rich with the scent of incense. The cacophony of sounds included drumming, singing, voices raised in joy and prayer, and the footfalls of troupes of dancers lining the streets. It seemed that every face in the crowd was lit by a smile.

Kundun's servants left the summer palace first, bearing the family's personal possessions and clothing, along with food and cookware so that they could immediately

make the family comfortable when they arrived. The most important lamas and state officials came next, providing another explosion of colorful material, including lush silk fabrics draped over their ponies. Porters carried ropes for the ascent to the Potala: located high on a hill, it was no simple task for all the people and baggage to reach it. Finally, eight monks in yellow hats gingerly carried the golden palanquin, from which Kundun peeked out through the golden curtains covering the windows.

Behind the palanquin came the regent, Reting Rinpoche, dressed in his most stunning finery, and Kundun's family, surrounded by abbots and tulkus in maroon and gold. The last man in the procession was the official doorkeeper of Potala's monastery, who did his best to keep the eager spectators from crowding too close.

The Potala loomed over Kundun, looking more like a small city than a palace. Seemingly endless staircases led from the ground level of the Potala square up a steep hill. The palace itself stretched into the sky—impossibly high, with a red central section and white wings flanking it on either side.

The procession passed beneath the carved snow lions that topped the massive red doors of the palace. Once inside,

Kundun must have noticed immediately how different the Potala was from the Norbulingka. While the summer palace was light and airy, the rooms and corridors of the Potala were cold, dark, and shadowy. Spectacular *thangkas*, paintings of deities on silk wall hangings, covered the walls. Precious and sacred objects, many of which were made of gold, were everywhere. But a permanent draft permeated most areas. Perhaps the chill would have been increased by the knowledge that in the farthest depths of the palace was a dungeon where criminals were imprisoned, rarely to be seen again. The dankness of the palace, with all its rooms and secrets, was a sharp contrast to the warmly comfortable summer palace. It took nearly 20 minutes for Kundun and his family to climb the stairs of the palace's 13 stories. Eventually, Kundun was brought to the private rooms on the top floor that would be his home for many years to come. With the official enthronement less than a day away, the boy needed to get all the rest he could.

Lobsang Samten would be living near Kundun as his companion, and having his brother nearby must have brought Kundun some comfort. But during the boys' first night at the palace, Lobsang was extremely frightened of the many dark corners in his room. The Potala's 1,000 rooms had no

Tibetan officials climb the Potala steps on the day of the enthronement, February 1940.

electricity, and butter lamps provided only a limited amount of light in large chambers with high ceilings. Lobsang asked one of the monks to sleep in the room with him but was told in no uncertain terms that he would spend this and every other night in the Potala sleeping alone.

Kundun himself had no difficulty falling asleep in his new quarters. He was not even disturbed to learn that he was sharing his bedroom with mice. A small altar occupied part of Kundun's sleeping chamber, and the mice scampered onto it to consume the food and water the boy had left as an offering to the Buddha. Kundun came to develop a great affection for his little roommates, even when they scurried over his blankets in the dark of night.

As the most important person in the palace, Kundun's quarters were naturally much larger and grander than those given to Lobsang. But even though they were the grandest private rooms in the palace, they were no warmer or brighter than any others. The furniture and heavy curtains appeared to have been gathering dust for several centuries. Kundun had a suite of four rooms, including a chapel. The chapel contained little statues and thangkas, and another room contained a small library of scriptures. But the chamber that both boys found most interesting was Kundun's bathroom, which consisted of a wooden chair with a fur-covered toilet seat placed over a hole in the floor containing a chamber pot. It was the only indoor bathroom in the entire palace. Lobsang probably hoped that as the Dalai Lama's brother and closest friend he would be allowed to use this exotic invention. He was heartbroken when Kundun told him that he would have to go down the 13 floors' worth of steps to the outhouse, just like everyone else.

WELL BEFORE DAWN THE NEXT MORNING, the palace was thronged with dignitaries. All of them had brought lavish gifts for the young god-king. Kundun was most interested in the gifts of Western origin, things he had never seen before, such as a cuckoo clock, binoculars, and a miniature car operated by foot pedals. All his life, Kundun would remain fascinated with mechanical objects and would indulge his interest by taking them apart and trying to put them back together again. Gifts that were small enough were laid out on a table in a room next to the Potala's main hall. They included a variety of jewels and precious metals, small statues of Buddha, a golden watch, a hammock, an English riding saddle, bolts of silk and other fine materials, holy books, a rhinoceros horn, and two live parakeets in a cage. The gifts that would not fit on the table included a pair of horses, a 6-foot elephant tusk, and the miniature car.

Hours after the dignitaries had assembled in the main hall, the call was made for silence. A white carpet was unrolled from the hall's entrance to the golden throne sitting at the other end of the large room. Trumpeters sounded a ceremonial call to attention.

All those present rose to their feet, the air thick with anticipation. The doors were thrown open, and the boy confidently walked into the room. He wore robes of gold and a pointed hat, and was flanked by two attendants, his small hands clasped tightly in theirs. Members of the crowd watched in reverent silence as the figure, less than half their size, strode down the length of the white carpet. When he reached the throne, he climbed up the steps to its base. But the boy was too small to get up into the throne without assistance. One of his attendants, Chikyab Khenpo, who was the most senior religious official of the government, lifted Kundun onto the throne. From his lofty seat, the apple-cheeked boy had a commanding view of the hall and its occupants.

The Lion Throne takes its name from the eight lions, carved of wood, that flank it. The wooden throne was constructed following directions given in a sacred Buddhist scripture, covered in a thin overlay of gold, and decorated with jewels. In keeping with the exalted status of the Dalai Lama, the throne towered 7 feet above the floor. The seat was comfortably furnished with five square cushions covered in brightly colored, embroidered silk. Next to the throne sat a table of gold decorated with rubies, turquoise, and pearls.

Kundun's family sat in a place of honor to the left of the throne. Perched on his cushions, Kundun towered over his family, and he would have had an excellent view of the top of his brother Lobsang's head. On his right was the Oracle of Nechung, no longer in a trance but sitting in reverent silence. Far across the hall, ministers and government officials sat facing their new leader. To the right, on the western wall, a long splash of crimson marked the robes of abbots, tulkus, and monks who were important enough to be invited to the ceremony. The eastern wall was lined with visiting dignitaries. All eyes were on Kundun.

Kundun watched in silence as the regent approached the throne and prostrated himself before the god-king. The regent pressed his hands together as if in prayer and touched them to the crown of his head, forehead, throat, and heart before lying on the ground and stretching his hands out in front of him. He repeated this three times. Then, in single file, the government officials and monks followed suit, approaching the throne and prostrating themselves before the newly discovered Dalai Lama, offering ceremonial gifts and receiving blessings. Kundun sat in silence, his face a mask of solemn composure.

To the assembled Tibetans, the enthronement ceremony that followed was not so much the greeting of a new leader, but a loving welcome home to a returning lord, now clothed in a different body, to resume the responsibilities he had temporarily left upon the death of the 13th Dalai Lama. The atmosphere of joyful excitement in the hall was electrifying.

Prayers were offered for the health and vitality of the Dalai Lama. This was only the first in a long string of blessings, prayers, and offerings that would occupy Kundun's next five hours. By all accounts, he never fidgeted or became distracted but remained focused at all times. Still, a dance interlude and the chanting procession must have been a welcome break from the long ceremony. Kundun watched the masked performers with interest as he sat on his Lion Throne, wrapped in silks against the chill. During the entertainment, Lobsang quietly climbed the steps of the throne to sit at his brother's feet and keep him company. During these moments, Kundun exchanged affectionate looks with his mother and father, and with friendly and familiar faces he picked out in the crowd.

Kundun sits atop the Lion Throne during his enthronement ceremony, February 22, 1940.

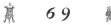

There were ceremonial tea rituals and feasting at the 50 tables set up in the hall to accommodate all the guests. Kundun drank tea poured from a golden vessel with a spout in the shape of a dragon. He was offered food of every kind and was always served first. There were pastries molded into edible sculptures, tsampa, pork, mutton and yak meat, breads, rice, and candied fruit and nuts.

After the feast, Kundun listened while two monks recited a prayer of long life and prosperity to the Dalai Lama and Buddhism. When the many verses had been recited, Kundun allowed his two attendants to lift him down from the throne. Hand in hand with the monks, the most celebrated child in all of Tibet left the palace's main hall to return to his quarters.

Witnesses commented on the extraordinary composure and self-confidence the boy had displayed during the long, tiring installation ceremony. They observed that he had never appeared bored or disinterested. This was just as well, because the next day a second wave of dignitaries would arrive, and Kundun would be required to attend another day of ceremonies, blessings, and ritual.

Kundun had a great deal to occupy his attention. But one of the things he most wanted to do was play with the many gifts and toys that were still arriving at the palace, particularly the parakeets. Kundun did not hesitate to use his new authority and sent a string of messengers to insist the two birds be delivered without delay to his quarters. The representatives of the British government who had brought the birds had intended to keep them for a while, to give them time to get used to their new living situation after what must have been an exhausting trip, even for birds. But there was no one willing or able to say no to the Dalai Lama's request, and soon they were delivered to him. Kundun immediately consulted the British representatives to learn everything he could about the care and keeping of his new pets. He kept a close watch on the birds whenever he was in his quarters, where he also kept his other favorite gifts—a cuckoo clock, a watch, and a music box. These three precious items sat in a place of honor on a table reserved for Kundun's personal property.

After the exhausting schedule of his first several days at the Potala, Kundun finally had some time to get used to his new living situation. His family had been installed in a pleasant stone house not far from the palace, and they too were taking time to adapt to their new circumstances. It took some effort for them to adjust to their new position as royalty. Far from the hours of labor required of a peasant woman living in Taktser, Diki Tsering now had a legion of servants, secretaries, maids, chefs, and even two people designated as vegetable cleaners. The Great Father, Choekyong Tsering, had always been passionate about horseback riding. He was presented with a number of magnificent horses, along with grooms and stable boys to care for them.

Diki Tsering remained the forthright, down-to-earth woman she had been back on the farm. The society and customs of Lhasa were sophisticated compared to those she had known in Amdo, and she was careful not to break any unwritten rules or throw her weight around. She treated her servants with great kindness and insisted that others do likewise. Though she received gifts of magnificent dresses and jewelry, she preferred to continue wearing the plain and sensible clothes she had brought from her farm. But she could not mother her son as she used to. His care was now in the hands of the monks.

Two official tutors had already been appointed to instruct Kundun, though he was too young to begin his official studies. The senior tutor was Reting Rinpoche, the regent who had overseen the search for the Dalai Lama and who intended to rule until the boy came of age. The second tutor was Kewtsang Rinpoche, the monk onto whose lap little Lhamo had climbed when the search party had come to Taktser. But until he was old enough, most of Kundun's interactions would be with his three primary personal attendants, who were also monks. His favorite was the Master of the Kitchen, a middle-aged monk named Lobsang Jimpa. Kundun called him Ponpo (Boss) and became so attached to him that he didn't like the monk to leave his sight. Kundun met Ponpo just days after arriving in Lhasa and often comforted himself when he missed his mother by climbing into the attendant's arms and pressing his lips to Ponpo's face. Ponpo played with Kundun whenever he could, and when he learned of the boy's fascination with Western-style pants, he fashioned a pair from an old shirt and some twine. The boy was delighted with his makeshift trousers. The fact that Ponpo was also the source of all of Kundun's meals, and occasionally produced a treat such as a lump of brown sugar, further cemented his position as a substitute mother and favorite of the young child. They would remain friends for the rest of Ponpo's life. Kundun also befriended the other room attendants, whom he called sweepers. Their job was to clean the rooms, fetch water, tend to the butter lamps, and keep all of the floors polished. Kundun eagerly waited for them to finish their work, because he loved to run and slide along the freshly polished floors.

While the resident monks of the Potala provided a daily rhythm of prayer, meditation, and devotional chanting, Kundun and Lobsang had a large measure of freedom and could more or less do as they liked. There was no end of rooms and halls to explore. Though there were miles of passageways, Kundun and Lobsang had no fear of getting lost—a pair of attendants quietly trailed them during all their explorations.

The boys soon discovered that the most comfortable and cheerful place to play was the roof. From there, they had an extraordinary view of Lhasa and the surrounding countryside. Kundun had found a telescope, which allowed him to watch the city's children playing. In time, he became particularly interested in a nearby prison and began watching the inmates in their daily walks around the grounds. He felt protective of them, and empathetic, particularly when he saw prisoners wearing cumbersome wooden collars as extra punishment. Occasionally one of the prisoners would catch sight of the boy, who was instantly recognizable even from a distance. The prisoners' response was no different from any other Tibetans'—they would immediately prostrate themselves three times to show their devotion and respect to the god-king.

When warmer weather came, Kundun and Lobsang moved back to Norbulinkga, the summer palace. It was a much better place for boys to amuse themselves and to get exercise in the lush gardens. But Kundun could not play forever. When he turned six, he would have to give up much of his playtime to begin his traditional studies and his religious education on a wide variety of subjects. He would also be extensively tutored in politics and matters of state.

There was an enormous amount to learn, and a multitude of monks and advisers were coming together to instruct Kundun in all that the highest living power in Tibet needed to know.

Palace of
One Thousand Rooms

ཁང་མི་ག་ཆེ་ག་སྟོང་ཅན་གྱི་ཕོ་བྲང་།

O<small>N JULY</small> 6, 1941, K<small>UNDUN</small> turned six years old, and the days of freedom came to an end. When he moved to the Potala that year, he began to follow a strict schedule of devotion and education. His day now began at six in the morning, when he rose and prayed and meditated for an hour. Kundun had no complaints about getting up so early—he was a naturally early riser. Not everyone could say the same. One early morning, Kundun sat with one of his attendants, while the Master of the Ritual began chanting his prayers in the next room. Kundun could hear the prayers clearly, as well as the dropping of the voice as the monk nodded off to sleep.

Kundun, approximately five years old, in an undated photograph

After a moment, the monk awakened and began chanting again, only to drop off to sleep again shortly thereafter. Kundun could not resist laughing. In the days that followed, he would discover that the Master of the Ritual quite frequently fell asleep during his morning prayers.

Every day, after eating breakfast, Kundun and Lobsang began their studies with the fundamentals: reading and writing. Kundun was also usually asked to learn and recite a Buddhist text. His studies were interrupted mid-morning for a meeting with government officials. The regent, cabinet members, and other civil servants would leave their offices in the Potala and go to the assembly hall. There, they held serious, structured meetings. Officials paid their respects to the Dalai Lama, then discussed the daily affairs of state and received briefs outlining their required tasks for that day. Kundun watched in silence. It was important for him to become familiar and comfortable with government proceedings, although it would be years before he took an official role in the meetings. According to tradition, he was not meant to become an active political ruler until he reached his majority at age 18. At that time, leadership would be officially transferred to him in a special ceremony.

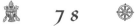

After lunch, Kundun and Lobsang had playtime, which, not surprisingly, was their favorite part of the day. Visitors often brought gifts to Kundun, and he had collected a number of toys and objects such as model soldiers. During playtime, the two brothers would share the toys or explore the 1,000 rooms of the Potala Palace, peering into dark chambers and occasionally marveling at what they found inside. Each room held something unexpected. There were treasures of the palace, religious artifacts, swords and armor, scriptures, and, most exciting, multitudes of crates containing gifts that had been shipped to the palace for the 13th Dalai Lama in the past decades. The boys greatly enjoyed these explorations, always supervised by the monks who followed them, and often would return to their rooms with some interesting souvenir of their expedition.

During these playtimes, the two came as close as they ever would to resembling a pair of normal brothers. One day, Kundun found an old walking stick and was swinging it wildly around when he accidentally clipped his brother in the head. To Kundun's horror, Lobsang dropped to the floor, unconscious. Blood poured from a gash over his eye. For a terrible moment, Kundun thought he had killed his brother. But, though bloody, the gash was not life-threatening. Lobsang made a full recovery, though the scar would always be visible.

Following playtime and lunch came several more hours of studies, including both religious and cultural subjects. The schoolroom was filled with sun during the late morning hours, but by afternoon it began to grow dark. Kundun hated the moment when the rays of sunlight left the schoolroom. He imagined that as the shade began to creep over the schoolroom, it also crept over his heart. During times like this, Kundun sometimes felt frustrated and closed in, as if he were in prison. He remembered hearing shepherds singing in the distance, strolling across the pastures toward their homes. From his darkened classroom, Kundun sensed the simple happiness of the shepherds, free to roam and sing outdoors, while he had to remain inside with his tutor.

Though his tutors found him to be highly intelligent and an unusually quick study, Kundun considered himself to be a reluctant student in those days. In his first year of study, he did not particularly like any of the subjects he was being taught. At times, it was difficult for him to behave. But the boys never forgot the two whips hanging on the wall of the schoolroom. The yellow one, they were told, was intended for Kundun. The other one was earmarked for his brother. Not surprisingly, the yellow whip remained on the wall at all times, but on several occasions Lobsang's whip was used. When Kundun misbehaved, no monk wanted to punish him. So when the tutors grew especially frustrated, Lobsang occasionally suffered on his brother's behalf.

At the end of the day, Kundun would wait for his tutor to leave so that he could go out on the roof to check in with the world through the eye of his telescope. After supper, more time for prayer was set aside, followed by bedtime.

Though the Great Mother was permitted to come to the Potala to visit her sons, as a woman, she could not remain overnight at the palace. Kundun had to be satisfied with daytime visits, during which his mother, like any other visitor, would bow down before her young son. Still, she would bring him treats and snacks and freshly baked bread, pampering him as best she could while still displaying the respect accorded a god-king. Though he had grown accustomed to living in the palace without his mother, Kundun would most certainly have welcomed more visits.

Diki Tsering had another son in 1943, when Kundun was eight years old. The baby died two years later when a smallpox epidemic swept Lhasa. Another boy, named Tendzin Choegyal, was born less than a year after the baby's death.

Kundun saw his father frequently, as the Great Father often attended the morning tea ceremony with the monks. (As a woman, Diki Tsering was not permitted to join in.) Other family members occasionally came as well, including his eldest brother Norbu, who had completed his first examinations at Kumbum and obtained permission to continue his studies in Lhasa.

But when visitors left the palace, the only family Kundun had was Lobsang. His three personal attendants, Master of the Ritual, Master of the Robes, and Ponpo, the Master of the Kitchen, remained close to the brothers and acted as older siblings or parental figures. But his best friend (and the only one near his own age) was his brother.

Lobsang was always a diverting playmate, but the brothers had the most fun together when they were staying at the summer palace. The birds and animals on the palace grounds provided endless entertainment to the boys.

Though Kundun and Lobsang were extremely close, they continued to argue. Lobsang was the more naturally peaceful of the boys, and Kundun tended to be more aggressive. He craved physical activity, and his favorite game was to set up a board at an incline, run up it as fast as possible, and leap off the top. To his dismay, the game was banned by his attendants. But there was always something else to do, with Lobsang at his side for solace, study, and play. Soon that was to change as well.

When Kundun turned 11, Lobsang was sent to a school outside of the palace, in part because the brothers squabbled so frequently. Kundun watched from a window as his brother was led away by an attendant. Periodically, Lobsang turned to get another glimpse of his brother—a tiny outline of a figure on the top floor of the palace—and the boys would forlornly wave to each other.

Now Kundun had no playmates his own age, though the sweepers were good company. They were known to indulge the boy in some legendary toy soldier battles, complete with wooden guns. They regaled Kundun with ghost stories, including a particularly frightening one about a room in the Potala haunted by a demon named Arko Lhamo. They also told him that people had seen

The view from the upper stories of the Potala Palace, 1936

spirits wandering the dim halls of the palace. He found the stories terrifying.

Since he could not wander the streets like a regular citizen, Kundun had to content himself with watching the goings-on in Lhasa through his telescope. He watched children playing, people walking and conducting business in the streets, all the aspects of a normal life of which he was not a part. One day, Kundun caught sight of herdsmen leading thousands of sheep and yaks to be slaughtered. He was so anguished at the prospect of their deaths that he sent an attendant down to the streets to buy all of them and spare them the slaughterhouse.

Constantly curious about the outside world, Kundun sought ways to learn more about it. During one of his now-solo explorations of the palace rooms, Kundun found a movie projector, powered by a hand crank, that had been a gift to the 13th Dalai Lama. There were several canisters of film, along with the projector. To Kundun's frustration, no one at the palace seemed to know how the projector worked. He would not give up, and eventually a monk was located who understood the mechanics of the contraption. The old monk was able to get the projector working, and Kundun eventually learned how to operate the machine for himself. He was fascinated by the films; particularly by one documentary about England's King George V. When the machine stopped working one day, Kundun could not get it started again. (By this time, the monk who had first gotten it working had died.) Kundun had to content himself with removing the projector's lightbulbs and dropping them out of the palace windows. He described the sound they made on impact as "lovely explosions." Eventually, someone was able to fix the projector, and new lightbulbs were obtained as replacements.

Around this time, Kundun learned of an unusual visitor to Lhasa: a German mountaineer named Heinrich Harrer

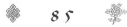

had come to the Holy City after a long and improbable journey. At a time when Tibet's borders were technically closed to all foreign travelers, the mountaineer, with his rugged build, blond hair, and blue eyes, quickly became a highly visible personality in the city. Kundun soon learned that Harrer knew a great deal about the outside world, including the mechanics of such exotic devices as movie projectors. He was eager to meet the stranger, but first the German had to pass muster with the Holy Family, making several visits to Diki and Choekyong Tsering, and Kundun's brother Lobsang.

Frustrating as these layers of protection must have been for a curious boy who longed to know more about the world, they served a real purpose. Kundun was still of

Heinrich Harrer, right, with a Tibetan official, in Lhasa, April 1954

great interest to the Chinese and was potentially a target for anyone seeking political power within Tibet.

In 1947, after returning to Lhasa after a day trip, Kundun's father developed sudden stomach pains. He grew sicker and more emaciated each day. By the end of the month, he was dead. Though he had not spent much time with his father as a child in Taktser, Kundun had received frequent visits from him at the palace. Choekyong Tsering's sudden death was a blow.

At Diki Tsering's request, her husband was cremated and his ashes returned to her in a wooden casket. The family then prayed for 49 days—the amount of time Tibetans believe the souls of the departed remain in their homes.

The cause of Choekyong Tsering's death was a mystery, though some of the family suspected that he was murdered. It seems unlikely that the family would have shared their concerns with 12-year-old Kundun, but one can imagine that rumors were circulating like wildfire through Lhasa. Kundun may well have caught wind of the suggestion that something was not right.

If the suggestion of foul play was accurate, what was the motive? The Great Father had not been as well liked as his wife. Unlike Diki Tsering, who remained relatively humble

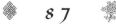

in her exalted position, Choekyong Tsering had undergone a change after coming to Lhasa and finding himself a wealthy and influential member of the royal family. Some people felt that he took unfair advantage of his new position. More importantly, Choekyong Tsering had become a friend of Reting, the regent who had played such a large role in locating the 14th Dalai Lama. Reting had stepped down as regent in 1941 in the face of rumors that he was dishonest, and a new regent had been appointed on his recommendation. However, Reting had returned to Lhasa after hearing Kundun's life might be in danger and had remained close with the Great Father. Both may have been looked upon with suspicion by the government, which was suffering from internal power struggles.

The fallout from Reting Rinpoche's resignation had rocked the palace. Kundun had been only six years old when Reting had stepped down among accusations of dishonesty. But in 1947, Kundun was 12, old enough to hear the whispers of gossip that accompanied Reting's return to Lhasa. His former regent and his current regent, Taktra Rinpoche, were locking horns. Shortly after Choekyong Tsering's death, a plot to murder Taktra went awry. The regent took swift action, and Reting was named as the man responsible. Taktra Rinpoche's supporters took up arms against Reting's supporters—Kundun saw the confrontation through his telescope from the roof of the Potala. For years, his sweepers had told him of the political infighting and backstabbing that went on in the government. Now he was witnessing it for himself.

Reting himself was not long for this world. After his supporters were defeated, he was thrown in jail. Though he requested that he be able to speak with Kundun, a representative would not grant the request. The Dalai Lama remembers peering out a window and watching his former regent being taken away. The fact that his present and former regent had taken up arms against each other saddened him greatly, but he knew there was nothing he could do to make the situation better. Reting died in prison shortly thereafter, possibly at the hands of his captors. Kundun sometimes wondered whether he could have stepped in to discourage the violence. But at age 12, he had no real political power.

Kundun had now experienced some of what it meant to be the Dalai Lama—the isolation, the long hours of study, the political plotting, the mysterious deaths. Even his regent, Tibet's temporary ruler until the Dalai Lama turned 18,

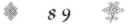

was not safe. And in far off Amdo, it was becoming all too clear how important a tulku could be as a political pawn.

The second highest-ranking lama and tulku in Tibet is called the Panchen Lama. The 9th Panchen Lama had died in 1937, and by 1944 several boys had been identified as his possible reincarnation. One of the boys, Gonpo Tseten, hailed from the Dalai Lama's home province of Amdo. The Chinese, believing they could influence Gonpo Tseten, hastily announced that he had been recognized as the 10th Panchen Lama, in spite of the fact that it is the Dalai Lama alone who has the authority to make this decision. The situation remained unresolved for several years, with the Chinese determined to establish their choice of Panchen Lama as a possible rival to the power and influence of the Dalai Lama.

It seemed that threats to the well-being of the Dalai Lama were lurking everywhere. Still, Kundun was content, always managing to find ways to amuse himself. Increasingly he anticipated the move to the summer palace each year. It was one of his favorite days.

The walled Norbulingka was sheltered from the outside world. By all accounts, it was a magical place. Hidden within its walls was a legendary park, home to a number of birds and animals, including deer, dogs, camels, peacocks, parrots, geese, leopards, a monkey, and a tiger. The more dangerous animals were kept in cages, but the others were free to roam the paths circulating through the gardens. As a young boy, Kundun had particularly enjoyed hand feeding the fish that swam in Norbulingka's lake, until one day he toppled in and had to be pulled to safety by an alert sweeper. The fish, which Kundun loved, became so tame over the years that they recognized his footsteps and swam to the surface when he approached. Kundun spent hours wandering through the paths, surrounded by flowers and trees. The soil at Norbulingka was said to be especially fertile, and vegetables grown there grew to enormous sizes.

When he was not playing in the gardens, Kundun eagerly listened to the sweepers tell stories of their lives,

The Norbulingka Palace grounds in 1936

relating all the injustices and pleasures experienced by a Tibetan of the working servant class. This connection to and interest in the lives and troubles of "ordinary" Tibetans was a quality Kundun would always have, and which would serve him well as a leader.

Teenaged Kundun also made time to tinker with the mechanical objects he had discovered packed away in the Potala. He was fascinated by the technology of other cultures, particularly European ones. He read a Christian magazine called *Tibet Mirror,* which reported on international news. The British Mission sent him issues of *Life* magazine, which he devoured. He was particularly interested in following the events during and directly after World War II. He began to teach himself some simple English from textbooks he had found crated up in a dusty room deep in the heart of the Potala. It was about this time that Kundun began spending more time with Heinrich Harrer.

Harrer had first glimpsed the Dalai Lama during a celebration of the Tibetan New Year. It was nighttime, and the streets were thronged with people waiting to see the Dalai Lama make his ceremonial ritual walk around the Parkhor Temple. Monks had worked for hours carving butter sculptures of deities, which were brightly colored and eerily lifelike in the soft glow of moonlight and butter lamps. Harrer watched along with the crowd as Kundun was escorted onto the street by two abbots. He was struck by the awed silence of the assembled people as they watched their god-king perform his ceremonial walk around the temple, as so many pilgrims visiting Lhasa did every year. Unlike the throngs of Tibetans surrounding him, Harrer did not share the belief that the boy at the center of all this attention was actually a living Buddha. Nonetheless, he was deeply moved by the reverence of the crowd and the obvious faith they displayed in the Dalai Lama and their religion. Harrer thought of the child not as a god-king but as the boy in the golden prison. Little did he know they would one day become friends.

When Harrer organized a skating club in Lhasa, Kundun soon heard about it and found he was unable to see the skating through his telescope from the palace roof. Through his family, he sent a movie camera to Harrer with instructions for him to film the skating so that Kundun could enjoy watching it. Before long, Harrer was being given other filmmaking projects for the young Dalai Lama, and soon he received his biggest assignment: the construction of a small movie theater at the summer palace.

When the theater was complete, Harrer met the Dalai Lama in person for the first time. Kundun was greatly amused by Harrer's blond hair and called him Gopse, which translated as yellow head. Harrer was struck with Kundun's overwhelming curiosity about the outside world—the boy had so many questions he could hardly get them out fast enough. They quickly became friends, with Harrer teaching Kundun all he wanted to know about Europe, geography, world events, and modern technology. When Kundun received an electric movie projector from the British government, Harrer helped him get a generator to power it.

A S H E G R E W O L D E R , Kundun became more and more interested in Western culture and political events. As always, he continued to be drawn to mechanics. He was particularly curious about three motor cars that were housed, though never used, at Norbulingka. One of them was an American car made by Dodge, and the other two were British Baby Austins.

Kundun knew that he was not supposed to go near any of the cars. So he cast about searching for someone who understood automobiles, finally locating and hiring a driver. The driver managed to get a couple of the cars running. Naturally, it was expected that Kundun himself would not tinker with the vehicles. But his insatiable curiosity overcame him.

One day when his driver was away, Kundun crept unobserved into the shed where the cars were kept. An ignition key was needed to start the Dodge, but the Baby Austins could be started by cranking a handle. Within minutes, Kundun had the engine of one of the Baby Austins started and was backing it out into the garden, where he happily chugged around the pathways until he was stopped, literally, by a tree.

To his dismay, he discovered he had broken one of the car's headlights in the impact. When his driver returned the next day, he would certainly notice the damage, and Kundun's secret expedition would be a secret no more. Determined to repair the damage himself, he found a replacement piece of glass and smeared it with syrup to make it resemble the original tinted glass. When his driver returned the next day, the man said nothing about the condition of the Baby Austin. Perhaps he hadn't noticed. Or perhaps the driver had simply decided to keep the incident to himself. In any event, it was the end of Kundun's brief career behind the wheel.

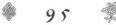

"The Red Onslaught at our Door"

ང་ཚོའི་གོ་འགྲམ་དུ་དམར་པོའི་དམར་གསོད།

T HE CARS THAT SO CAPTIVATED Kundun had belonged to the 13th Dalai Lama, considered to be one of the greatest Tibetan leaders in history. In addition to modernizing and reforming Tibet, he was a remarkable visionary and was keenly aware of the threat China represented. At the time of his death, he had feared that Tibet's darkest days were close at hand. Kundun would soon learn how right his predecessor had been.

In 1910, the Chinese had invaded with the intention of making Tibet an official province of China. The 13th

Chinese Communist leader Mao Tse-tung surveys his troops after defeating Nationalist forces in Beijing, China, 1949.

Dalai Lama had fled to India but returned a year later to what he proclaimed was an independent Tibet. In the decades that followed, China's attention had been diverted from its neighbors by a civil war, waged between the Chinese Communist Party and the Chinese National Government. When the Japanese invaded China in 1937, Chinese focus turned more fully from Tibet to their own country.

At the time of Kundun's birth in 1935, Chinese influence in Tibet was limited to small border territories such as Amdo. Several Chinese officials lived peacefully in Lhasa, where they had established a radio station. Kundun's older brother, Gyalo Thondup, had even been permitted by Tibetan officials to go to China to study the language in 1946. In spite of China's continued insistence that they had a legitimate claim over Tibet, no major conflict occurred between the two countries during Kundun's first 13 years. Tibet was self-governing and functioned independently. However, in 1949, the year Kundun turned 14, the relationship between China and Tibet rapidly deteriorated.

In the last testament he wrote before his death, the 58-year-old 13th Dalai Lama made some ominous statements. He began by foretelling his own death in the near future. Then he went on to make dire predictions about Tibet's relationship with China saying, "In particular we must guard ourselves against the barbaric red communists, who carry terror and destruction with them wherever they go. . . . It will not be long before we find the red onslaught at our door . . . when it happens we must be ready to defend ourselves. Otherwise our spiritual and cultural traditions will be completely erased . . . . The Monasteries will be looted and destroyed, and the monks and nuns killed or chased away . . . all of our cultural and spiritual institutions persecuted, destroyed, and forgotten . . . and the days and nights will pass slowly and with great suffering and terror." As events unfolded, many of his predictions would come true.

In 1949, Chairman Mao Tse-tung inaugurated the Communist People's Republic of China after defeating the Nationalist Party in the Chinese civil war. The era of the Chinese Communist Party, or CCP, had begun. Part of the CCP's ideology was a deep-seated hostility toward religion, and Tibet was uneasy. When Tibet suffered a colossal earthquake in August 1950, it was universally interpreted as a bad omen. At the Norbulingka palace, the Dalai Lama felt the floor rumble beneath his feet. He heard reports of more ill omens coming in from across Lhasa. Loud explosions had been heard from the direction of the northeast, and an unusual red glow had illuminated the skies. Mountains had been leveled. Even his friend Heinrich Harrer could not explain the phenomena, other than relating the events to some kind of aftershock.

One day soon after, a messenger rushed into the palace with a letter for the regent. Kundun peered through a small window into the room where the two men met. As the regent read, his face betrayed intense worry. Kundun later learned the content of the letter: Chinese soldiers had attacked a Tibetan border post. Kundun was overwhelmed by sadness and worry. As it turned out, his concerns were well founded.

In October, news reached the Potala that 40,000 Chinese soldiers of the People's Liberation Army had crossed into Tibet to carry out their mission, ironically and inaccurately described as the "peaceful liberation" of the country from "imperialist oppression." Tibet's tiny army was almost immediately squashed, and some 5,000 of their soldiers killed. The People's Liberation Army was headed for Lhasa, and the situation was grave. Though the young Dalai Lama was not supposed to be given his official ruling power until he turned 18, the oracle advised that it must happen immediately. The prospect deeply worried Kundun. He felt he knew far too little about the outside world and had virtually no political experience. But he also understood that in this time of despair, only one person could unite the Tibetan people. As the one who had been officially recognized as the 14th reincarnation of the Dalai Lama, he was that person. Not much more than a month after the CCP invasion began, the official transfer of political power was scheduled to occur.

One of the first provinces invaded was Amdo. Kundun's oldest brother, Norbu, now called Taktser Rinpoche, had returned there and had become abbot of the Kumbum Monastery. Once the territory was overrun by the CCP, Norbu was kept under tight watch at all times. Two Chinese soldiers remained with him wherever he went. The CCP attempted to "reeducate" him to make him view Chinese Communist policy favorably. Norbu found himself exhausted and in despair over their daily attempts to convert him to their antireligious way of thinking.

Deeply concerned that his position as brother of the Dalai Lama could bring harm to his beloved monastery, Norbu reluctantly resigned as abbot. But the CCP kept up their intense efforts to bring him over to their side, insisting he travel to Lhasa to persuade his brother to adopt a pro-Communist viewpoint. Should he be unable to change the Dalai Lama's position on the matter, Norbu was told to kill him. Should he be unwilling to make the trip to Lhasa, Norbu's own life would be in danger. Given the choices, Norbu chose to pretend that he had accepted the CCP position and was willing to make the attempt to convert his brother. Any other appearance, he believed, would have resulted in his imprisonment or murder.

When Norbu reached Lhasa, Kundun barely recognized the anxious and stammering man as his older brother. He could plainly see that Norbu had been through a terrible ordeal. Norbu told Kundun that he had pretended to go along with a CCP plan to convince the Dalai Lama to support the Chinese, or have him murdered. The young Dalai Lama gasped in shock. Most of what he knew about the Chinese had come from magazines—this was his first direct experience with the Chinese Communist Party's hatred of religion, and the lengths to which they were prepared to go to subdue Tibet. Norbu told the Dalai Lama what had been going on in Amdo. Monasteries were being plundered of their sacred artifacts and burned. Land was being redistributed and monks forced into manual labor. Spiritual practices such as the burning of incense and butter were condemned as useless and wasteful. Violence against the people was occuring with increasing frequency. In spite of their many years of peaceful and contented existence, citizens of Amdo had been informed that Buddhism was the source of their "miserable condition."

Norbu told his brother he now believed that armed resistance and assistance from foreigners was Tibet's only hope. Norbu urged his brother to leave Lhasa at once. Norbu himself now intended to renounce his monk's vows and leave Tibet to seek help from the outside world. Kundun was unable to talk his brother out of his plan. Saddened and shaken, Kundun knew he did not have the luxury of indulging his own emotions. Important events were at hand.

Several days later, a ceremony was held to officially transfer power to the Dalai Lama. Kundun marked the occasion by ordering the release of all the prisoners from

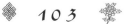

the jail near the Potala, the old friends whom he had watched for hours through his telescope. This, at least, was something positive and compassionate that he could do for his people. The 6 million citizens of Tibet were facing the most catastrophic threat in their history, and 15-year-old Kundun was now their leader. The weight of the responsibility was enormous, and Kundun knew that all eyes were now on him.

One of Kundun's first acts as Dalai Lama was to send delegates to America and Great Britain seeking help. An appeal was also made to the United Nations. When word reached Lhasa that Tibet's UN appeal had been dismissed and that no help was coming from America or England, it was devastating. Tibetans understood that they would receive no military or diplomatic assistance. Years of isolation and aversion to foreigners were now taking a toll on Tibet. The country was on its own. The Dalai Lama considered this the most bitter lesson Tibet had yet to learn.

Members of the Tibetan government began to urge the Dalai Lama to get out of Lhasa while there was still time. Part of the palace treasure of gold and silver was secretly transported to the country of Sikkim. Unable to get help or to defend themselves, there seemed no alternative but

The Tibetan delegates on their way to China, November 1950

to begin a dialogue with the Chinese Communist Party. Several delegates were sent to Beijing, and at the same time arrangements were hastily made to remove the Dalai Lama to a remote town near the Indian border. The Holy Family, with the exception of Lobsang, had already left Lhasa. Lobsang was extremely ill at the time, and when Kundun's party departed, they carried Lobsang with them on a stretcher. They left in the dark of night, with 200 Tibetan soldiers for protection. Just over two weeks later, they arrived in Yatung, a Tibetan village not far from the Indian border.

There were some bright moments for Kundun during this time. His brother's health greatly improved, and the

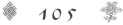

two were able to take long walks together in the remote countryside. They waded in streams, ran after butterflies, and played games together, just as they had as children in the summer palace.

This brief period of happiness came to an abrupt end when Kundun heard an announcement on the radio that the delegates from Lhasa had signed a document in Beijing called the Seventeen Point Agreement. The document effectively agreed that Tibet would willingly become part of China. The Dalai Lama was stunned. The delegates had not been given the authority to sign any treaty. It was later discovered that they had been told that if they refused to sign, the People's Liberation Army would overwhelm the country by force.

Some people, including Norbu and Heinrich Harrer, advised Kundun to leave Tibet immediately and seek refuge in India. He was the most influential and beloved leader in Tibet, and the CCP might likely imprison or even kill him. Others urged him to return to Lhasa and work with the Chinese. It was a difficult period of indecision for Kundun, but he ultimately decided to stay and face the Chinese. When word reached Yatung that a Chinese general was on his way to meet the Dalai Lama, Kundun prepared himself for the encounter.

His first reaction to the general was surprise that this representative of his ferocious enemy looked just like any other human being. The meeting was polite, if nothing else. The general provided Kundun with a copy of the Seventeen Point Agreement and made it clear that the Chinese wanted Kundun to return to Lhasa. He also gave reassurances of the spirit of friendship in which the Chinese had come to Tibet. Kundun had little choice in the matter. Soon afterward, the Dalai Lama prepared to return to Lhasa.

He arrived home with his entourage in August 1951, after an absence of nine months. Several weeks later, 3,000 Chinese troops marched into Lhasa, waving the People's Liberation Army flag and banners carrying the image of CCP leader Mao Tse-tung. From the Potala roof, Kundun watched the long columns of soldiers marching into Lhasa. By the end of the year, the number of troops occupying the Holy City had increased to 20,000. It seemed that by returning to Lhasa, Kundun had jumped out of the frying pan and into the fire. But there is an old Tibetan saying that when one is burned by fire, one must then heal by fire. The source of Tibet's troubles was the CCP government and troops, and it was to them that the Dalai Lama would now look for a peaceful resolution.

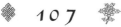

"Religion is Poison"

ཆོས་ནི་དུག

FACED WITH THE OVERWHELMING FORCE of the People's Liberation Army, the Dalai Lama felt utterly helpless. Being forced to work with the Chinese Communist Party was not a pleasant prospect. But resistance could bring disaster—Tibet's citizens looked to the Dalai Lama for guidance. Kundun was still just a teenager, and the stress and anxiety of the recent events weighed on him heavily. Feeling conflicted and cornered, he appealed to his senior tutors for advice. They reminded Kundun that it was his birthright to serve the Tibetan people and that the time had come for him to take on this awesome responsibility. They encouraged and supported

The Dalai Lama (right) with Chairman Mao Tse-tung and the Panchen Lama (left) in Beijing, 1954

him as best they could, but for Kundun it was a lonely time. He knew that if he appeared uncooperative the Chinese army might well resort to widespread violence. Sooner or later, Tibetans would begin to fight back, continuing the cycle of bloodshed. There were already several resistance groups springing up throughout Tibet, among them the Tibetan Freedom Fighters, who conducted small raids and surprise attacks against the invaders.

In the first months of Lhasa's occupation, the Chinese soldiers were cordial, even friendly to the Tibetans. They maintained that their presence in Lhasa was an act of friendship and that their ultimate desire was to bring assistance and positive change to Lhasa. But the atmosphere soon changed.

The burden of feeding the 20,000 soldiers was on the people of Lhasa, and after a time there was simply not enough food to go around. As conditions worsened, pockets of resistance began to spring up in and around Lhasa. Small armed groups of Tibetans attacked Chinese soldiers when they could. The people of Lhasa began to speak openly of their anger at the People's Liberation Army, demanding they go home. Children threw rocks at the soldiers. A Chinese general decided that two of the Dalai Lama's top ministers were responsible for the deteriorating attitude in Lhasa and ordered that they be dismissed. He summoned the Dalai Lama and demanded that he personally forbid Tibetans from criticizing the People's Liberation Army in any way. The first year of CCP occupation gave way to a second, and a fragile if unhappy balance was struck. When the Dalai Lama was invited by Chairman Mao to visit China in 1954, he agreed to go.

Many Tibetans feared that if the Dalai Lama did go to China he would never been seen again. Kundun was still hopeful that he could develop a real dialogue with the Chinese government, and it was in this spirit that he traveled to Beijing. However, underlying his desire to talk peace was the knowledge that realistically, he had no choice. Chairman Mao had asked to see him, and the only acceptable answer was yes.

Kundun was now 19, and this was to be his first visit to what he considered the outside world. In spite of the circumstances, he was excited at the prospect of what he might see. He traveled with an escort of close family members, including his mother, his oldest sister Tsering Dolma, and brothers Lobsang Samten and Tendzin

Choegyal. Also coming were a number of tutors and other official attendants. The group was treated to a tremendous farewell ceremony as they left the Norbulingka Palace and assembled at the Kyichu River. The party numbered close to 500, and the crowd was estimated in the tens of thousands. The sounds of music were amplified over the water, mingling with the scent of incense and the voices of countless Tibetans who had gathered there to wish their leader a safe journey.

On the banks of the river, the party divided into little groups to be ferried across the water in small yak-hide boats. Kundun crossed in a special boat, or coracle, twice the size of the others. An attendant accompanied him, holding a large red umbrella so that his shaved head would not become sunburned. When Kundun turned back to give the crowd a final wave, he was heartbroken to see that many of them were in tears, and more than a few had become distraught. They clearly believed that they might be seeing their Dalai Lama for the last time, and there was nothing Kundun could to do reassure them of his safety.

The distance from Lhasa to Beijing is approximately 2,000 miles. Kundun must have been delighted to learn that he would be traveling the first part of the

journey in one of his three cars, which had been floated across the river on a raft. However, he enjoyed this luxury for less than 100 miles. The road that the Chinese had been building had been washed away, and the party soon switched to mules and horses. Conditions were treacherous. Landslides caused debris to rain down around them. Young Chinese soldiers attempted to protect the travelers by creating a barrier between the Dalai Lama's group and the path of the landslides. In doing so, three Chinese soldiers were stuck by falling rocks and killed.

In some places, they passed groups of Chinese prisoners laboring to unearth the road by hauling away loads of boulders and rocks. These were the unfortunate who had been arrested during the Chinese civil war, or during Mao's recent land reforms when farms were taken from those considered wealthy and given to peasants.

It was rough going for a full month, until the road conditions improved and they were able to use jeeps that had been sent to meet the party. The countryside had changed since Kundun last traveled through it. Chinese houses and military barracks had been built, and in towns and villages troops had mounted loudspeakers through

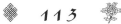

which pro-Chinese announcements celebrating the glory of the Motherland constantly blared. After crossing the border into China in his jeep, Kundun had his first plane ride. In spite of his preoccupation with politics, he was excited and fearless during his short time in the air.

The final leg of the journey to Beijing was made by train. The 12-hour trip was another first for Kundun. His youngest brother, eight-year-old Tendzin Choegyal, was overwhelmed by the train, which contained different cars for dining, for sleeping, and for sitting. Tendzin was particularly impressed with the quality of food in the dining car.

In Beijing, Kundun was joined by the Panchen Lama, who was several years younger. The Chinese insisted the Panchen Lama be there, to demonstrate that he was of equal status and influence to the Dalai Lama, something all Tibetans knew to be untrue. The two had lunch together and got along well. The Panchen Lama had been in China for many years and was considered by Tibetans to be little more than a pawn of Mao's government. In fact, the Chinese had recently announced that their Panchen Lama was being named chairman of a provisional Tibetan government. Official Tibetan acceptance of this tulku had come only by virtue of the Seventeen Point Agreement. Nonetheless, the Panchen Lama showed enormous respect to Kundun and behaved in a traditionally Tibetan manner. It seemed to Kundun that without the constant oversight of the Chinese, this young tulku might well have been an ardent supporter of Tibet's independence.

Chairman Mao Tse-tung was sixty-one years old when the Dalai Lama met him in September 1954. By the time of Mao's death in 1976, it would be estimated that he was responsible for the deaths of more than 25 million people. His plan to transform China from a society of farmers to an industrial force, known as the Great Leap Forward, resulted in a famine that wiped out the population. The Cultural Revolution was also engineered by Mao to transform China by erasing its cultural heritage and fostering Communism. This included widespread destruction of art and literature and the imprisonment or execution of China's leading artists, scholars, and intellectuals. Kundun knew nothing of this side of the chairman. He knew only that Mao was an incredibly powerful leader and that all China bent to his will.

The two came face-to-face at a banquet in Beijing's House of Reception. The Dalai Lama and Chairman

Mao shook hands as rows of photographers focused bright lights on them and snapped picture after picture. Kundun's initial impression was of Chairman Mao's intensely magnetic personality, and that his handshake conveyed enormous self-confidence. Those first minutes were cordial and friendly. Over the next two months, many other meetings followed, some informal, and some at large official dinners. The Dalai Lama grew optimistic, impressed by the Communist Marxist principles of equality and justice for all people. It seemed, in theory, that this quality of Marxism which seemed to embrace fairness to all humans, rich and poor, was in keeping with the Buddhist philosophy of compassion and reverence for all beings. Kundun began to believe there really could be a peaceful resolution between the two nations.

But during their final meeting, Mao leaned close to the Dalai Lama and whispered, "But of course, religion is poison." Mao matter-of-factly explained that Tibet was an example of a country that had been poisoned by religion, and this was the obstacle that prevented Tibet from thriving.

As the spiritual ruler and highest-ranking religious figure in Tibet, the Dalai Lama did not know what to

make of the chairman's statement. He felt a deep sense of fear. For the past 10 weeks, Mao had reassured him that the CCP was sincere in its desire to help the people of Tibet. But religion was central to Tibetan life. Now it was understood that no matter what assurances Mao had made, he meant to destroy Tibetan Buddhism.

On his way back to Lhasa, the Dalai Lama's party stopped over at Taktser. Kundun was thrilled at the prospect of being reunited with friends and relatives he had not seen since he was four. But his excitement quickly turned to dismay. Poverty and unhappiness had come to Taktser. There were soldiers everywhere. Tibetans who approached Kundun were carefully watched. Even Diki Tsering was not able to converse with her old friends and neighbors until they had been interrogated by soldiers as to what they intended to talk about. The Chinese would not permit the Holy Family to eat any food prepared by their former neighbors—they allowed Kundun and his family to consume only food certified by a Chinese doctor. It pained Diki Tsering greatly that she was not permitted to accept such basic hospitality from her people.

The people who greeted Kundun all made almost identical statements about their happiness under

Communist rule. But as they did so, Kundun noticed their eyes filling with tears. He realized with horror that his former neighbors and friends were so fearful of Mao that they felt they must repeat pro-Communist sentiments, even to the Dalai Lama himself. Everywhere soldiers were eavesdropping. Most chilling was the absence of certain friends and acquaintances. These were the missing Tibetans, who were said to have been "deported," or to have died under circumstances that no one could or would explain.

People wore tattered, old clothing and seemed to be

Chinese vice-premier Chen Yi (center), the Panchen Lama (right), and the Dalai Lama review troops in Lhasa, 1956.

living in utter poverty. When Diki Tsering went to visit the family's former farmhouse, she had mixed feelings. At the family's request, Kumbum monks had been supervising the building of a new home, since Diki Tsering's family had grown. She had planned one day to return and live in this house with some of her family. Now it seemed impossible that would ever happen.

In May 1955, to the great relief of the people of Lhasa, the Dalai Lama safely returned to the Holy City. But the streets were not as Kundun remembered them. Everywhere he looked, he saw Chinese army military vehicles blocking the streets. In the past, the arrival of the Dalai Lama in the Holy City had brought throngs to the street, singing and dancing, and burning incense. But what greeted Kundun were trucks and soldiers, and the smell of exhaust fumes. The news reaching Lhasa from the rest of Tibet was also grim. More and more, Kundun was hearing reports of property being taken from individuals, random executions, and an organized campaign of violence and terror leveled at monks and nuns. When local Tibetans resisted, they paid a catastrophic price.

The following February brought the worst news to date: Chinese army troops had bombed a monastery, killing

119

thousands of Tibetan Freedom Fighters gathered inside. Devastated at this news, the Dalai Lama sent appeals to Chairman Mao for the kind of assistance he had offered in their many talks. Mao had promised that Tibet's government would be reformed with the input of the Tibetan people. He had assured the Dalai Lama that the core intent of all Chinese action in Tibet was to be helpful. The Dalai Lama now appealed for that help. But he received no reply.

It would be many years before the Dalai Lama learned that the Tibetan Freedom Fighters were secretly being trained and armed by the U.S. Central Intelligence Agency (CIA). Though America was not willing to go to war over tiny Tibet, they were interested in fighting Communism, considered the number-one enemy of democracy at the time. A CIA team, under the code name Operation ST Circus, recruited Tibetan resistance fighters and flew them to secret locations to train them in weapons use, explosives making, mine laying, and other war tactics. The team also provided them with guns. When the teams of Freedom Fighters were fully trained and provided with weapons and radios to communicate with the CIA, they were secretly parachuted back into Tibet. The program would last until 1979, when the CIA abruptly ended its support due to American diplomatic developments with China.

T HE YEAR 1956 BROUGHT the anniversary of the Buddha's birth. Indian prime minister Jawaharlal Nehru invited the Dalai Lama and the Panchen Lama to attend a celebration. The CCP did not want Kundun to leave Lhasa, but after a telegram from Nehru himself, the Communist authorities reluctantly allowed him to go to neighboring India.

When Kundun arrived with brothers Lobsang and Tendzin Choegyal, he was reunited with Norbu, who was living in India. And there was a surprise. His brother Gyalo Thondup had previously fled China, where he had been studying Chinese, in 1947. He had traveled the world since then and had been in the United States when he heard a rumor that the Dalai Lama would be visiting India. Gyalo Thondup instantly booked passage to Calcutta, India, and his presence completed the reunion. The five brothers were now together for the first time in Kundun's life. They were able to spend an entire evening together in the cottage housing the Dalai Lama, sitting around a table and talking by a roaring fire. There was

much to be said about family and politics. Norbu and Gyalo urged their brother not to go back home but rather to stay in India. They believed it was far too dangerous for the Dalai Lama to return to the explosive atmosphere of Lhasa.

Diki Tsering and daughters Tsering Dolma and Jetsun Pema had also traveled with Kundun. The family took advantage of this extraordinary opportunity to have their photograph taken. It was the first and only picture ever taken of the entire Holy Family. Only their father, dead now for nine years, was missing.

It was a joyful time for Kundun, but everywhere there were reminders of his political problems. When he traveled to Gangtok, India, he rode in a car flying a Tibetan flag. He was greeted by a joyful crowd of schoolchildren who tossed flowers in his path. The celebration was interrupted when a Chinese official ran to the car, tore the Tibetan flag away, and tied a Chinese flag in its place.

During his three months in India, Kundun and members of his family visited many of the most sacred Buddhist sites there. Kundun was able to go to Rajghat, where the ashes of his hero Mahatma Gandhi had been scattered. There he took some time to pray on the lush green lawns overlooking

The Holy Family in Delhi (left to right): Diki Tsering, Tsering Dolma, Thubten Jigme Norbu, Gyalo Thondup, Lobsang Samten, the Dalai Lama, Jetsun Pema, and Tendzin Choegyal

the Jamuna River. As he prayed, he felt a deep sadness that he would never come face-to-face with this extraordinary man who had sacrificed so much in the name of peace. But he was grateful for the example Gandhi's life made to both the world and to Kundun personally. He could not help but wonder what advice Gandhi might give to him were he alive. He suspected that Gandhi would urge peaceful action at all costs.

His brothers continued to urge Kundun to request asylum in India. He seriously considered it but was torn by the idea of leaving his people in such a helpless situation.

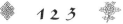

Still, when Kundun met Prime Minister Nehru, he brought up the subject with the Indian leader. He was surprised and disappointed to find the prime minister unsupportive. Nehru made it clear that he expected the Dalai Lama to act in keeping with the Seventeen Point Agreement—which meant the Dalai Lama should return to Tibet and work with the CCP. Ultimately, Nehru gave priority to maintaining a good relationship between India and China.

When Kundun prepared to return to Tibet, it was a deeply emotional time. He had known that neither Norbu nor Gyalo Thondup would be accompanying him to Lhasa. But Lobsang Samten, Kundun's brother and best friend, had also decided to remain behind in India. Though Lobsang had not lived with him in the palace for many years, he had always been nearby in the Holy City, and the brothers saw each other frequently.

Kundun returned to Lhasa without him. For the first time in his life, he did not have Lobsang nearby for comfort or counsel.

By 1959, the situation in Tibet had reached a boiling point. All pretext of winning over the Tibetan people had long been abandoned. Now, in villages and monasteries throughout the country, brute force was being used to bend the people to the Communists' will. The well-known prophecy of the 13th Dalai Lama, that "the days and nights will pass slowly and with great suffering and terror," were being borne out daily. As Tibetans grew angrier at the People's Liberation Army, Kundun heard of a chilling memo sent from Mao to the PLA advising that, if necessary, every Tibetan in the country could be thrown in prison.

In March of that year, Kundun received an invitation from the political commissar, General Tang, to attend a theatrical performance at a nearby Chinese military camp. The conditions placed on the invitation were suspicious. The Dalai Lama would be required to come to the camp without his usual group of 25 bodyguards, soldiers, and attendants. There would be no "ceremony" attached to the visit. The underlying meaning was clear—the Chinese wanted the Dalai Lama to come to them alone and unprotected.

Kundun did not openly reject the invitation, but it was obvious that he would have to proceed with extreme caution. The usual catch-22 was in place: if he accepted the invitation it was likely he would be putting himself in danger. If he rejected the invitation, he would be defying the CCP and therefore putting himself and every Tibetan in Lhasa in danger. As it happened, Tibetans who had heard of the suspicious invitation took matters into their own hands.

On March 9, 1959, the day before Kundun was to visit the Chinese camp, he was in his summer palace. As the sun rose, all seemed quiet and well. The rising sun illuminated the lake and the gardens of Norbulingka with a rosy glow. On the roof, a gentle breeze rippled through the prayer flags. Though he would only realize it much later, this was the last peace of mind Kundun would have for a long, long time.

That evening, a crowd began to gather outside Norbulingka's walls. Throughout the night and continuing through the morning, thousands of Tibetans joined the throng. By the middle of the day, nearly 15,000 people were surrounding the palace. Their purpose was simple— to put themselves between the Dalai Lama and the People's Liberation Army. The crowd refused to allow any Chinese near the palace, and an official suspected of being a Chinese spy was even killed by the mob. The events prevented Kundun from attending the theatrical performance, which infuriated the Chinese. They saw it as a blatant and dangerous act of defiance, but after so many years of CCP occupation, the fury of the Tibetan people was exploding.

Kundun knew there was no turning back. The uprising of March 10 changed everything. Though he had maintained his efforts to work with the CCP peacefully for almost 10 years, Kundun now accepted that his life, while he remained in Lhasa, hung by a thread. He also feared that the massive crowd protecting him would be slaughtered by the People's Liberation Army. In the midst of all this chaos, one thing became clear: it was time for the Dalai Lama to flee Tibet. Whatever Nehru had told Kundun about working with the Seventeen Point Agreement, the situation had now changed. Lhasa was in revolt, and the life of the Dalai Lama was clearly in danger. There would be no reconciliation with the Chinese. With the mobs of citizens and soldiers thronging the palace grounds, and Chinese authorities seething with anger, it could only be hoped that it wasn't already too late.

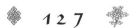

"Go! Go! Tonight!"

འཕེབས། འཕེབས། དོ་ནུབ་འཕེབས།

THAT NIGHT, THE HOLY FAMILY received an unexpected visit from one of Kundun's servants, who told them to discreetly pack a few belongings and go to Norbulingka. Over the next several days, tensions in Lhasa were high. Some of the crowd, satisfied that the Dalai Lama would not be going to the Chinese camp, went home. But many thousands remained. Announcements blared over the CCP loudspeakers extolling the virtue and power of China and comparing the Tibetan crowds to ants scratching at the feet of elephants. General Tang sent a letter to the

Tibetans rebels surrrender to Chinese forces outside of the Potala Palace, 1959.

Dalai Lama's senior ministers, instructing them to remove barricades the crowds had erected on the road toward China. The last letter to reach Kundun was from another senior Chinese general, advising him that Chinese troops planned to launch shells at Norbulingka. The Dalai Lama should advise them of the exact location of his personal palace quarters, the general suggested helpfully, so that the troops would know to aim away from them.

Kundun twice consulted the oracle and both times was advised to remain where he was. But as days passed and the situation grew more and more dire, he consulted the Oracle of Nechung again. This time, the oracle shouted frantically that His Holiness must not only flee, but that he must go that very night. Lurching unsteadily in full trance, the oracle then scrawled on a piece of paper the exact route Kundun must take to safely escape. An attendant monk, also a medium, dropped to the ground in a faint. Outside the palace, two shell explosions in the distance provided a booming endorsement of the oracle's urgent demands. The more time that passed, the more likely it would be that news of the flight would leak out to the public. If Kundun had any chance of making it out of Lhasa alive, no one, including his own staff and palace guards, must know what he meant to do.

Kundun had little time to indulge his regret at leaving the monks, attendants, and sweepers who had been his family for two decades. He took a brief moment to visit a shrine to Mahakala, a protective deity, where he watched the monks in the room chanting and tending to the butter lamps. Though he knew that it could hint to the monks in the room that he was about to flee, he placed a white kata scarf around the statue of Mahakala as a farewell symbol and took a moment to pray and meditate in silence. Kundun turned and left the shrine abruptly.

He dressed quickly in the uniform and fur cap of a Tibetan soldier and slung a rifle over his shoulder. Then, with darkness as his cover, he simply walked out of Norbulingka's gates, unnoticed by the crowds. He knew it might be the last time he would ever see his beloved summer palace.

The danger was greatest at that moment. There were Chinese soldiers everywhere in the streets, and violence could break out at any time. Kundun needed to reach the designated meeting place across the river, where he would rendezvous with his family and his closest tutors and attendants.

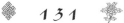

With the Lord Chamberlain, head of the royal household, and his chief bodyguard, a terrified Kundun made his way through the streets. His bodyguard spoke quietly to him, urging him to keep close. Because he had removed his glasses to further hide his identity, it was difficult to see clearly. But he could sense the enormous numbers of people gathered there. Among the crowds, rumors had already begun to spread that His Holiness planned to flee Lhasa later that night. Kundun kept his head down and tried his best to look like a soldier as he crept past the PLA patrols.

At the river crossing, Kundun and his two aides stepped into a coracle. When the boat reached the opposite riverbank, he was reunited with his immediate family members who still lived in Lhasa—his mother, his youngest brother Tendzin Choegyal, and his oldest sister Tsering Dolma. His mother and sister were both dressed in soldier's clothes. With the Holy Family were several ministers and tutors, all huddled together in the darkness. There was also a small contingent of Freedom Fighters and some ponies.

The little group departed in complete silence. PLA patrols were everywhere, and in this location, so close to

Norbulingka, lay the greatest danger that they would be discovered. To their right, only a few hundred yards away, was a well-lit group of tents. Kundun chose that moment to put his glasses back on. The sight of the Chinese military camp made him regret that decision. It was a misty night, however, and Diki Tsering believed that the fog helped to conceal the fleeing family. The clatter of the ponies' hooves on the stones seemed deafening, but the party passed the camp undetected.

Several miles from Lhasa, the countryside grew dark. After hours of traveling, Kundun could see a dim light from a small house in the distance. One of the party went ahead to discreetly inquire who lived there. When he discovered it was a lone and sympathetic Tibetan man, the official requested that an "important visitor" be allowed to rest there. The man must have been astonished to learn the identity of this visitor. Though it put his life at risk to shelter the Dalai Lama, the Tibetan agreed without hesitation. Indeed, they would come across many Tibetans who wanted nothing more than to offer aid to the party, no matter what the ultimate cost.

By dawn the next day, they reached a 16,000-foot pass over the mountain Che-La. Here the group paused, for

this was the last time that Lhasa would be visible. Kundun surveyed the Holy City in silence and then climbed off his pony to pray. From such a distance, the city looked serene and unchanged, as it had been in much happier times. There was nothing to say, and no time to waste. Kundun climbed back onto his pony.

Once safely beyond the mountain, the party made a cautious approach toward the Tsangpo River. There was only one ferry crossing, and the group could only hope that the Chinese had not guessed their route and awaited them there. To their relief, the ferry crossing was deserted, but to the Great Mother the sound of the ponies' hooves crunching over the gravel seemed to sound a thunderous alarm.

On the far bank of the Tsangpo, a group of Tibetans had gathered. Somehow they had learned or guessed that the Dalai Lama and his party would be passing this way. Many of them were in tears, and Kundun thought of how these same people had lived peacefully for many generations. Now all of that had been clouded over by fear for the future and terrible reports of PLA aggression.

After 18 hours of continuous travel, the party stopped at a small monastery to rest. While there, the Dalai Lama tried to get word to the Panchen Lama that he was in the process of fleeing Tibet. He urged the Panchen Lama to consider escape. Kundun knew the odds were not good that the letter would ever actually reach its intended recipient—he could only try.

At the monastery, they were joined by a Freedom Fighter who had a transmitter and was constantly sending Morse Code updates to his American CIA operatives. Kundun recognized the Morse-key transmitter, but he was never told, nor did he ask, who was receiving the messages. There were new arrivals from Lhasa, as well, and the number of men escorting the group had now increased to almost 400. Though there was some safety in numbers, the group also knew that the bigger it got, the harder it would be to slip past Chinese troops unnoticed.

They got underway early the next morning, climbing up to another mountain pass, where they struggled through a blizzard. Many of the travelers were not at their strongest or most fit—the Great Mother was 70 years old. But time was of the essence, and it was impossible to slow the pace to accommodate everyone. If they sacrificed speed, it could mean their capture.

Day and night they continued, pushing themselves to the limit of their capabilities and seeking shelter in homes

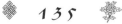

or small monasteries at night. After many days of this grueling travel, a small group of men on horseback caught up with the party, bearing devastating news. PLA troops had advanced on Norbulingka, machine-gunning the crowd and launching artillery attacks on both palaces, the Jokhang Temple, and all the major monasteries. Thousands were dead, and many of the most sacred buildings in Lhasa had been reduced to rubble. Kundun's beloved Norbulingka was nearly destroyed. Houses had been set afire. The messengers said that the Chinese had not at first realized the Dalai Lama had escaped. Teams of soldiers combed Lhasa to find him before they realized that he had fled.

Kundun was stunned. The worst possible outcome had occurred. The PLA had begun to slaughter his people and lay their temples and homes to waste. And Kundun could only wonder: Why? Why had they done it?

But he knew why. The Tibetans had asserted themselves. And through love of the Dalai Lama and of their religion, they had the audacity to openly defy the Communist government. They had paid dearly for it. There was nothing Kundun could have done for his people. Had he remained at Norbulingka he would most likely already be imprisoned or dead.

All hope now lay to the south and the border between India and Tibet, more than a week's hard travel ahead. But first the group stopped at a fort called Lhuntse Dzong, 60 miles from the Indian border, where a small crowd of officials and monks was waiting to receive them. It was relatively safe there, but they were not yet home free. By now, the Chinese knew that the Dalai Lama was making for the border with all possible haste.

The Dalai Lama took the opportunity at Lhuntse Dzong to make a formal statement rejecting the Seventeen Point Agreement. A brief religious ceremony was held to bless the newly established temporary government of Tibet. A small group of officials was dispatched to the Indian border to make arrangements in advance for the Dalai Lama's arrival.

Soon they were under way again. The closer they got to India, the more difficult travel became, but they had heard reports of Chinese activity in the area and had to press on. They encountered snowstorm after snowstorm, and their eyes and fingers grew numb in the freezing wind. There had been no time to pack such luxuries as extra clothes, and the group struggled against the bitter wind and snow with no added protection for their heads, feet, and hands.

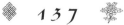

As Kundun and his escorts reached the highest point of the final mountain pass between Tibet and India, they heard the hum of a low-flying airplane above them. In the brilliant white snow, there was nowhere for the people to conceal themselves. The plane flew directly over the frightened group, and there was no question that the pilot had seen them. If the plane was Chinese, then their location was no longer a secret. Though they were in a remote area and couldn't be reached by roads, the PLA could easily dispatch additional planes to attack them by air. But there was no sense in pondering how or when an attack might happen. All they could do was plod on, ignoring their exhaustion.

They stopped again in Mangmang, the last village in Tibet before the Indian border. Official word had been radioed from India that the Dalai Lama had permission to enter the country. But overnight the weather took another bad turn. It began to rain heavily, and Kundun's tent leaked all night. By morning, he was running a high fever. His condition was so serious that they were unable to move on, in spite of the possibility that Chinese planes could return at any time.

The next day, Kundun was still too weak to get on a horse. However, his attendants were able to get him onto a large work animal called a *dzo*, a Tibetan yak-cow hybrid.

The animal's back was wide and flatter than a horse's, and its gait slow and smooth. With enormous sadness, Kundun said good-bye to the soldiers, bodyguards, attendants, and Freedom Fighters who had accompanied him on the most difficult journey of his life. He had known some of them for years, and some of them for just days, but Kundun was deeply affected by the bravery and devotion every one of them had displayed in escorting him to the border. After assisting the Dalai Lama in his flight from Tibet, they would now face even greater danger from the Chinese. Kundun feared they faced almost certain death. Clinging to the animal, still dazed by fever and exhaustion, Kundun was borne out of Tibet and away from the people and land that he loved more than life. He knew that, in this lifetime at least, he might never be permitted to return.

Epilogue

མཇུག་གི་བཙོང་ད།

THE EXILED DALAI LAMA and his group were welcomed into India. They established a community and government in exile in the mountainous village of Dharamsala, where it is still located today. The news of his 1959 flight, sometimes called one of the "great epic stories of the twentieth century," was heard around the world. When Mao Tse-tung learned that the Dalai Lama had reached India safely, he said, "In that case, we have lost the battle."

In the 50 years that have passed since His Holiness fled Lhasa, Tibet has endured its darkest hours. The Chinese Communist Party worked to eliminate Tibetan Buddhism and destroyed 90 percent of all monasteries

---

A young Tibetan monk protests in Nepal, March 2008.

in the country. By 1980, only eight monasteries and 1,000 monks were thought to remain in Tibet. The Tibetan government-in-exile estimates that more than 1.2 million Tibetans were killed or died from torture or starvation during the Chinese purges. Citizens were required to take an oath of allegiance to the CCP and to adopt Chinese dress and language in place of their own. Thousands of sacred scrolls and religious artifacts were destroyed.

After the death of Mao Tse-tung in 1976, it seemed the worst might have passed. During the next decade, some of Tibet's destroyed temples and monasteries began to undergo restoration. Some measure of personal liberty was returned to the people and more latitude given to private lifestyles. But the persecution and mistreatment of Tibetans has continued. Seventy percent of Tibetans live below the poverty line. Property development has destroyed much of the pristine countryside, and more than half of Tibet's magnificent forests have been cut down, causing soil erosion and flooding. The Buddhist ban on hunting was lifted, and now more than 80 Tibetan species are endangered. China continues to send its citizens to live in Lhasa, where Chinese now outnumber native Tibetans. Except for the towering presence of the Potala, present-day Lhasa is virtually unrecognizable. Monks, nuns, and civilians are still arrested and jailed, often for years. It is against the law to distribute or even carry a photograph of His Holiness the 14th Dalai Lama.

In March 2008, following a peaceful commemoration of the 1959 uprising, there was an outbreak of protests in Lhasa against Chinese rule. Chinese police quickly moved in, arresting and reportedly beating protestors. In the ensuing chaos, violence was committed by Tibetans and Chinese alike, and deaths occurred on both sides. The Chinese crackdown was swift. Military police closed all roads to the city and sealed off and surrounded the region's three most important monasteries. Protests continued to spread across the Tibetan plateau. Though things had changed since 1959, the cycle of protests and military reprisals was familiar. When the 2008 Summer Olympic Games took place in Beijing, China, the eyes of the world turned to Tibet. Rallies supporting Tibet were staged around the world. The Dalai Lama reiterated his desire to dialogue with the Chinese. He released a letter containing an appeal for peace and friendship to the Chinese people, whom he addressed as his brothers

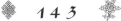

and sisters. In America, an Internet petition requesting that the Chinese address human rights violations in Tibet and agree to dialogue with the Dalai Lama gathered 1.5 million signatures. At the time of this writing, both strife and hope endure in Tibet.

The Dalai Lama, throughout the decades, has continued to work tirelessly on behalf of his people, both those in Tibet and those living in exile. His goal in the early twenty-first century is to obtain self-government for his people and personal and religious freedom for his country. The Dalai Lama has repeatedly maintained that he bears no hatred toward those who attacked and violated his people. He sees all people—regardless of their nationality—as human beings who share one goal: to be happy and to avoid suffering.

The Dalai Lama's view that all people are alike is a crucial part of his story. He does not view the Chinese people as enemies. Theirs is a proud and distinguished culture with an extraordinary history. They have suffered more than their fair share of persecution throughout history, both from their own government and from outside forces. The invasion of Tibet began as the handiwork of an exclusive group of men under Chairman Mao, whose policy was to expand the rule of the Chinese Communist Party through force. As ruthless as Mao was in his treatment of Tibetans, he was even more brutal to millions of Chinese during the Great Leap Forward and the Cultural Revolution. As is so often the case, it is the masses who suffer when an elite few misuse their power.

Today, the Dalai Lama is a world-famous leader who travels the globe. He visits with political and religious figures and speaks to the public about the plight of the Tibetan people, and about the universal religion of compassion. He also visits the many Tibetan refugee camps that have been established for Tibetans who continue to flee their native land. His representatives continue to periodically meet with Chinese delegates. His consistent efforts to obtain a peaceful resolution for the Tibetan people have not gone unnoticed. In 1989, the Dalai Lama was presented with the Nobel Peace Prize, the highest and most prestigious award of its kind. In October 2007, he was awarded a Congressional Gold Medal which recognized his dedication to the Middle Way approach to achieving a peaceful resolution with China. The Dalai Lama's vision will no doubt continue to guide the people of Tibet as they struggle to win genuine freedom.

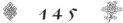

In one of his books, Western Buddhist teacher Jack Kornfield relates an anecdote about the Dalai Lama. A friend of Kornfield's described attending a lecture the Dalai Lama was giving at New York's Madison Square Garden. An exquisite and ornate throne had been set up onstage, where His Holiness would sit. When the Dalai Lama walked up the steps and sat down on the throne, he discovered that beneath the beautiful silk fabric were mattresses intended to make the seat as comfortable as possible. Kornfield writes:

> When the Dalai Lama sat down on the throne, it bounced. A smile lit his face. He bounced again, and smiled more. Then, in front of thousands of students, before offering the highest teachings on the Wheel of Time and the creation of the world, the Dalai Lama bounced up and down as happily as a child.

Seven decades have passed since two-year-old Lhamo Thondup was discovered by a search party in the remote village of Taktser. His life today as an international religious leader, revered and honored throughout the world, is as far removed from his first few years as can be imagined.

And yet, Kundun retains the innocent happiness of a child.

His Holiness, the 14th Dalai Lama

Selected Bibliography

Bell, Sir Charles. *Tibet Past and Present*. Delhi, India: Motilal Banarsidass Publishers, 1992.

Chhaya, Mayank. *Dalai Lama: Man, Monk, Mystic*. New York: Doubleday, 2007.

Craig, Mary. *Kundun: A Biography of the Family of the Dalai Lama*. Washington: Counterpoint, 1997.

David-Neel, Alexandra. *My Journey to Lhasa*. Boston: Beacon Press, 1927, 1993.

Diemberger, Maria Antonia Sironi. *Tibet: The Roof of the World Between Past and Present*. Vercelli: White Star Publishers, 2004.

Farrer-Halls, Gill. *The World of the Dalai Lama*. Wheaton, IL: Quest Books, 1998.

Goodman, Michael Harris. *The Last Dalai Lama*. Calcutta, India: Rupa & Co., 1996.

Harrer, Heinrich. *Seven Years in Tibet*. New York: Jeremy P. Tarcher/Putnam, 1953, 1996.

Hilton, Isabel. *The Search for the Panchen Lama*. New York: W.W. Norton & Company, 1999.

His Holiness the Dalai Lama. *Freedom in Exile: The Autobiography of the Dalai Lama*. New York: HarperPerennial, 1991.

His Holiness the Dalai Lama. *My Land and My People*. New York: Warner Books, 1962, 1997.

His Holiness the Dalai Lama. *My Tibet*. Berkeley and Los Angeles: University of California Press, 1995.

Kornfield, Jack. *After the Ecstasy, the Laundry.* New York: Bantam Books, 2000.

Laird, Thomas. *The Story of Tibet: Conversations with the Dalai Lama.* New York: Grove Press, 2006.

Morgan, Tom, ed. *A Simple Monk: Writings on His Holiness the Dalai Lama.* Novato, CA: New World Library/Tibet House, 2001.

Mullin, Glenn H. *The Fourteen Dalai Lamas: A Sacred Legacy of Reincarnation.* Santa Fe, NM: Clear Light Publishers, 2001.

Norbu, Thubten Jigme. *Tibet is My Country.* New York: E.P. Dutton & Co., 1961.

Strober, Deborah Hart, and Gerald S. Strober, ed. *His Holiness the Dalai Lama: The Oral Biography.* Hoboken, NJ: John Wiley & Sons, 2005.

"Tibet Press Watch, Spring 2008." Washington, DC: International Campaign for Tibet, 2008.

Tsering, Diki. *Dalai Lama, My Son: A Mother's Story.* New York: Compass Books, 2000.

Wangdu, Khemey Sonam, Sir Basil J. Gould, and Hugh E. Richardson. *Discovery, Recognition and Enthronement of the 14th Dalai Lama: A Collection of Accounts.* Dharamsala, India: Library of Tibetan Works & Archives, 2000.

Online Resources

Official Website of His Holiness the 14th Dalai Lama: www.dalailama.com.

Official Website of the Central Tibetan Administration of the Tibetan government-in-exile: www.tibet.net

Office of Tibet in New York: www.tibetoffice.org.

The Tibet Fund: www.tibetfund.org

Tibet Aid: www.tibetaid.org

Tibet House: www.tibethouse.org

Acknowledgments

I'd like to specially acknowledge and thank the following people:

My outstanding editor, Deirdre Langeland
Marcia Wernick
Lobsang Nyandak
Tenzin Deyang
Marnie Hillsley
Edmund Eng
Ghala Khamba and Tibetan Arts & Crafts, Woodstock, NY
Pattie Traina and Many Light Hands, Cold Spring, NY

My eternal thanks, respect, admiration, and friendship to Dr. Kathleen Nolan of Tibet Aid, Woodstock, NY, for assistance, guidance, and inspiration well above and beyond the call of duty.

Grateful appreciation to the Office of His Holiness the Dalai Lama.

Lastly, I have inexpressible gratitude for this opportunity to connect with the history and teachings of the Dalai Lama, and offer thanks for the generous words he wrote for this book, the inspiration he provides, and his unshakeable force of love and compassion. May His Holiness the Dalai Lama enjoy health, vitality, peace, and long life.

Photo Credits

Index

About Tibet Aid

TibetAid is an international relief organization dedicated to providing humanitarian assistance to Tibetans in Tibet as well as those living in exile. The organization's vision is to see Tibetan culture, traditions, and religion remain alive and flourish. TibetAid's Tibetan Sponsorship Project links individual sponsors with specific Tibetan children, nuns, monks, and elders. Other TibetAid projects include programs building, staffing, and supporting Tibetan schools and medical clinics on the eastern Tibetan plateau, and the Precious Seeds Fund for Children, supporting Tibetan preschool, primary, and secondary education, as well as Tibetan cultural activities for children.

For more information, please visit www.Tibetaid.org.

TIBETAID

• TIBETAN SPONSORSHIP PROJECT
• RURAL TIBETAN SCHOOLS & HEALTH CARE
• MEDICAL RELIEF FOR TIBETAN REFUGEES
• ANNUAL TOUR TO TIBET
• PRECIOUS SEEDS FUND FOR CHILDREN

Dedicated to providing humanitarian assistance to Tibetans in Tibet and in exile. Our vision is to see the culture and traditions of Tibet and its people remain alive and flourish.